# *Periodic Chart of Virtuous Living for Teens*

## ONE ELEMENT AT A TIME

# REV. FRED R. GAGLIA, PH.D.

outskirtspress

DENVER, COLORADO

# ACKNOWLEDGMENTS

Every reasonable effort has been made to determine copyright holders of excerpted materials and to secure permissions as needed. If any copyrighted materials have been inadvertently used in this work without proper credit being given in one form or another, please notify the author in writing so that future printings of this work may be corrected accordingly.

Unless otherwise noted, the Scripture citations used in this work are taken from the *Revised Standard Version of the Bible* (RSV) Revised Standard Version of the Bible, copyright 1952 [2nd edition, 1971] by the Division of Christian Education of the National Council of the Churches of Christ in the United States of America. Used by permission. All rights reserved.

Abbreviations used for biblical quotations:

D-R    Douay-Rheims
ESV    English Standard Version
KJV    King James Version
NAB    New American Bible
NAS    New American Standard

NASB  New American Standard Bible
NIV   New International Version
NJB   New Jerusalem Bible
NKJV  New King James Version
NRSV  New Revised Standard Version
RSV   Revised Standard Version

NIHIL OBSTAT:
Mr. James-Daniel Flynn
Censor Deputatus

IMPRIMATUR
Most Reverend Samuel J. Aquila, S.T.L.
Archbishop of Denver
April 18, 2013

# DEDICATION

*TO MY MOTHER AND FATHER*

The gift of life for me was made possible by the shared love of my mother Marie and my dad Fred. They were the source of my first training in the faith and the ones who developed it in my childhood. They were my constant support and encouragement in life. Their prayers and sacrifices were the foundation of my vocation and responsible for my perseverance. May they look down from heaven, appreciate the results of their prayer and sacrifice in this book.

# CONTENTS

# PREFACE

Blessed John Henry Cardinal Newman once wrote, "to live is to change, and to be perfect is to have changed often."

In an age of skepticism where nearly everything is called into question, it is important to understand that faith and reason are not mutually exclusive, that people of strong religious faith have much to contribute to the world of science and technology. This is particularly evident in the lives of young people. There is an obvious need today to have a balance of developing spiritual growth and change in our young people, and the power of the technological age in their lives.

With "Periodic Chart of Virtuous Living for Teens -- One Element at a Time," Fr. Fred Gaglia has provided a way for young people to have a spiritual and moral parallel to their study of science and technology. It is a way to enkindle and motivate their search for the virtuous life, by relating concepts of the periodic chart with their growth in the spiritual life.

This book provides a way for students to get practical applications of virtuous living as they are studying the chemical elements in science classes. It can also teach them a new avenue of reflection on God's incredible gift of creation. It will make a good companion to go along with their science books.

Building an educational program on the virtues using the elements found in the periodic table is a very creative and compelling concept. I have never come across anything quite like this before. I have no doubt this work is the fruit of much prayer and years of experience with youth ministry on the part of the author.

The world is changing all around us. God is our one constant. The more we understand the world around us, the more we can make sense of the permanent things in life.

Bishop James D. Conley
Bishop of Lincoln

# INTRODUCTION

You run into in your high school biology or chemistry classroom for the first time . There on the wall is this huge chart of boxes. A mystery indeed. What is it for? Do I have to learn what it means? It is the periodic chart of elements. This chart was developed in its first published form in 1869 by Dmitri Mendeleev.

You may not have found it exciting but at least it is very challenging. I found it to be an exciting adventure into the order of nature. This became clear to me when I was studying for my degrees in biology. When I went into teaching biology, it became even more exciting. As a priest biologist, I found the periodic chart a wonderful expression of the order and adaptability of nature at the chemical level as well the order God has established in His dealing with us on the spiritual level.

It is well established that structure and order are hallmarks of living things. It is so ordered that when we talk of compounds (substances made from combination of elements) we see the incredible abilities of various elements. After many years of teaching this excitement of the beauty and order of God's creation, I began to see a relationship of this order of the elements into groups and functions as also a function of the order and functions of humans for their spiritual growth.

I became intrigued by the names of elements with each one given a symbol that made it easier to identify it. These symbols became the shorthand for chemistry. A whole shorthand then developed by which we could use those symbols, and the number of times an element is used, to write chemical formulas for various compounds. How neat is that for another expression of order in nature.

This intrigue has led me to make another application of the periodic chart of elements. After a lot of reflection, I wondered if I could take the symbols of the elements of nature, which gives us a pattern of order, and apply them to another pattern of order in our lives as children of God. The idea that these symbols could be used, by metaphor or analogy, as symbols of another order in our lives. That order would be the way in which we can live virtues. Thus was born this present work of taking the symbols of the natural elements and then using those same letters to have an application to virtues for living an ordered spiritual life. My focus is teens who use this chart. This may be a helpful tool not only to learn the elements of nature, but also the elements of virtues for their lives.

If attention to these virtues is done on a one at a time approach, a teen could grow incredibly in virtue over the years of high school. My approach is to try to make some comments on the call of the element in nature. Try to see some connections, when possible, of the elements to a virtue with the same letters as the element. Next, I try to support the virtue with references to God's Word, the Bible. Finally to give the student a challenge in how to apply that virtue to their lives.

The approach of this book, as regards the use of the Bible, is that the references to the scriptures be short quotations from God's word. This follows the common method that many of the saints used in their writings. This is best illustrated in the Church's Liturgy of the Hours where, in the Office of Readings, the writings of the saints follow this methodology. These short quotations have the purpose of being that, short, so that the reader can find a few words of inspiration and then possibly even be able to memorize these short texts. These texts are not meant to be in any form biblical exegesis, but a method to show that the concepts of the elemental virtues are found in the inspired word of God. Therefore, this is not a question of deliberately trying to quote out of context, but to give inspirational words for growth. I leave the task of exegesis to others. If the readers are inspired to search deeper into the quotations from the Bible they can refer to many good bible commentaries available.

The groupings of the natural elements is the basis for what we will loosely call "chapters" of my presentation to young people. The periodic chart of chemical elements is traditionally divided into periods and groups. The Periods (like Periodic table) are made up of rows (going left to right on the table, see appendix A). Each row is a different period. The groups are the columns of the Periodic table (going from top to bottom). All of the elements in a column have similar properties. Elements in the periods and groups have similar chemical properties. The final general division of the Periodic table are families.

These elements are grouped because of similar chemical properties. There are generally recognized nine different families of elements. We will use this division of families to establish the chapters for this book. We will list in each of those families the chemical elements in them and then give the comparative spiritual element to live by in those same families. Families is also a more familiar term for the spiritual life. We all belong to the family of God.

I have also provided a number of indices for a variety of uses for readers. In addition, even though the focus is primarily teens, the concepts can also be applied to adults.

I pray that this project is a blessing to the readers and that the Lord will grant a special blessing of growth in virtue to those who try to become virtuous one element at a time. You are ready for the journey, now begin and be blessed.

On this journey, you can do it in several ways. One journey might be to go from element number 1 to element 92. I have only treated of the naturally occurring elements in nature. Take one element a week or maybe if you are really getting virtuous you can do two a week.

Another journey might be to go through the elements in their groups as chemical elements, for example go through the elements of virtues like the grouping in the periodic chart of chemical elements. For example, you could take the noble gas group: Helium; neon; argon; krypton; xenon and radon. Look for those numbers in the virtue list and make that journey of growth. Finally another journey might be to refer to these spiritual elements when you are studying the chemical elements in one of your sciences classes. When you study hydrogen look and study this element, represented as holiness, in this present book. See God's instructions about the virtue of that symbol. It may even help you to remember the chemical properties in a more interesting way. God blesses you twice.

Remember that on your journey you will be reading the language of God in nature and in your spirit as a redeemed son and daughter of God. May these elements of life help you to aspire to be a saint.

Fr. Fred R. Gaglia, Ph.D., KCHS

# 1

# THE JOURNEY THROUGH GROUP 1, THE ALKALINE METALS.

The chemical elements of the alkaline metals are known as group 1 on the Periodic Chart. Although hydrogen in the Periodic Chart is not considered as an alkaline metal, it is in group 1 and so is included in this chapter. The group one elements, and alongside them, the spiritual elements of virtue in this chapter are:

CHEMICAL ELEMENT:          SPIRITUAL ELEMENT OF
                           VIRTUE:

Number: Name: Symbol

| | | | |
|---|---|---|---|
| 1 Hydrogen | H | **H**oliness |
| 3 Lithium | Li | **Li**ght |
| 11 Sodium | Na | **Na**vigate God |
| 19 Potassium | K | **K**indness |
| 37 Rubidium | Rb | **R**ighteous **b**eing |
| 55 Cesium | Cs | **C**hristian **s**trength |
| 87 Francium | Fr | **Fr**iendship |

#1 **H** = Hydrogen = **H**oliness:

## THE CALL

Like Hydrogen, which is the most abundant atom on the planet. Holiness is the most abundant gift we can strive for in our lives. For the teen it is not an easy task in a world set against holiness. Therefore, the Lord gives us the call to holiness. Strange as it is hydrogen the number one element is also the simplest and lightest of all the elements and the most abundant element in the universe. That should also be the makeup of our spiritual life, that is, holiness should be the simplest thing in our complex world and the most abundant element of our relationship with God. Also interesting is that we as humans are made up mostly of water. You guessed it water is two parts hydrogen and one part oxygen. It is obvious that without water we would not be much, but because we are seekers of holiness we are more than water that makes up most of our human bodies. As water is essential to who we are as mere humans so is holiness essential to who we are as creatures of our loving God. Let us examine what God's word instructs us about holiness.

## THE WORD OF GOD SAYS...

Leviticus 19:2 (RSV)
[2] "Say to all the congregation of the people of Israel, You shall be holy; for I the LORD your God am holy.

1 Thessalonians 4:7 (RSV)
[7] For God has not called us for uncleanness, but in holiness.

Psalm 93:5 (RSV)
[5] Thy decrees are very sure; holiness befits thy house, O LORD, for evermore.

2 Corinthians 1:12 (RSV)
[12] For our boast is this, the testimony of our conscience that we have behaved in the world, and still more toward you, with holiness and godly sincerity, not by earthly wisdom but by the grace of God.

Ephesians 4:24 (RSV)
[24] and put on the new nature, created after the likeness of God in true righteousness and holiness.

Hebrews 12:14 (RSV)
[14] Strive for peace with all men, and for the holiness without which no one will see the Lord.

THE CHALLENGE

There is nothing more exciting that seeing holy young people. I remember an occasion, at one parish I was assigned to, to witness young teens coming in on a Friday or Saturday night after athletic events, to come to the adoration chapel and spend some time before the Lord. What a dedication to living in holiness. What a preparation for the coming of heaven. What a witness to other teens to make holy all that they do in their lives. The next time you are going on a date or coming home from an athletic event, find a church near you that has perpetual adoration. Stop there, pray before the Lord for a time, and thank Him for something special that has happened in your life that week. If you cannot think of anything you can always thank the Lord for the gift of life.

## #3 **Li** = Lithium = **Li**ght

### THE CALL

Light is who Jesus says He is. He calls us to be light. Lithium, the number 3 element is interesting. Exposed to light it tarnishes. Just the opposite with the Lord, isn't it? In His presence we are called to radiate His light to others. If you have the light of Jesus you will not tarnish anything. If you see the Light, you will be the light. That is a great call of the Lord.

### THE WORD OF GOD SAYS...

Psalm 27:1 (RSV)
[1] The LORD is my light and my salvation; whom shall I fear? The LORD is the stronghold of my life; of whom shall I be afraid?

Psalm 97:11 (RSV)
[11] Light dawns for the righteous, and joy for the upright in heart.

Matthew 5:14 (RSV)
[14] "You are the light of the world. A city set on a hill cannot be hid.

Luke 11:34 (RSV)
[34] Your eye is the lamp of your body; when your eye is sound, your whole body is full of light; but when it is not sound, your body is full of darkness.

John 1:4 (RSV)
4 In him was life, and the life was the light of men.

John 8:12 (RSV)
12 Again Jesus spoke to them, saying, "I am the light of the world; he who follows me will not walk in darkness, but will have the light of life."

2 Corinthians 4:4 (RSV)
4 In their case the god of this world has blinded the minds of the unbelievers, to keep them from seeing the light of the gospel of the glory of Christ, who is the likeness of God.

1 John 1:5 (RSV)
5 This is the message we have heard from him and proclaim to you, that God is light and in him is no darkness at all.

THE CHALLENGE

There is enough darkness in the life of a young person these days. There does not have to be that darkness. One needs to seek the Lord and reflect the Lord to others to be light. It is like a lighthouse, where the lens reflects an inner light that brings help to others outside itself. The lighthouse light goes well beyond itself and is meant to assist others. What an image for a young person. Try to reflect inner light, that is the Lord present in you, to help direct your peers to a better "light filled" life. Center your own life in Jesus. You need His strength and source of truth to survive today. Make a decision today to reflect each day to one person an image of light that you have learned of Jesus in your life.

#11 **Na** = Sodium = **Na**vigate toward God

## THE CALL:

Sodium's symbol Na stands for its Latin root natrium. Since sodium is necessary for nerve function in animals, it helps them navigate the route a nerve impulse should take. It is the same for you to navigate in the world, you need to do it with God and in God's way. When one navigates, or is directed to God, one will have a clear path or direction to be a good person. As a side note, it is interesting to note that the importance of sodium as salt in the diet was recognized well before sodium itself was understood to be an element. This recognition formed the basis of trading of the salt deposits lining the Dead Sea in biblical times by the Romans.

## THE WORD OF GOD SAYS...

Acts 10:22 (RSV)
[22] And they said, "Cornelius, a centurion, an upright and God-fearing man, who is well spoken of by the whole Jewish nation, was directed by a holy angel to send for you to come to his house, and to hear what you have to say."

Sirach 49:9 (RSV)
[9] For God remembered his enemies with storm, and did good to those who directed their ways aright.

## THE CHALLENGE

If you navigate life with God, you cannot go wrong. It is not a possibility since the Lord always leads you in truth. What more can you ask from God? The difficulty is that you need to follow His navigation, His directions for your life. In a sense this is the way to heaven. He invites us to follow Him in faithfulness and this can make us reach our destination without frustration. Too much of your world is filled with frustration and so if you had a way of getting through those frustrations with a sense of security that God provides, why not follow it! Look each day for the ways in which the Lord wants to lead you in His ways. Try getting an insight into His ways by reading the Bible every day.

#19: **K** = Potassium = **K**indness

## THE CALL

This is an interesting element, we call it potassium. This element is essential for nerve and heart function. We give it a symbol of K. Let that K in the chemical world stand for another K in the spiritual world, namely kindness. Kindness is essential for your heart to be set on the desires of the Lord. Let us build on that symbol "K" and understand the need for Kindness in your world today. Teens have not been known to express outwardly kindness for one another or adults in their lives for fear that they will be made fun of. Strange is it not for this to be such a controller of a teen's behavior. Remember that kindness was such a mark of how the Lord interacted with people of His time.

## THE WORD OF GOD SAYS...

Proverbs 21:21 (RSV)
[21] He who pursues righteousness and kindness will find life and honor.

Micah 6:8 (RSV)

[8] He has showed you, O man, what is good; and what does the LORD require of you but to do justice, and to love kindness, and to walk humbly with your God?

Galatians 5:22 (RSV)

[22] But the fruit of the Spirit is love, joy, peace, patience, kindness, goodness, faithfulness,

1 Peter 2:3 (RSV)

[3] for you have tasted the kindness of the Lord.

Sirach 12:1 (RSV)

[1] If you do a kindness, know to whom you do it, and you will be thanked for your good deeds.

Sirach 3:14 (RSV)

[14] For kindness to a father will not be forgotten, and against your sins it will be credited to you;

## THE CHALLENGE

If you have an interest in history you may be excited to read what the ancient document known as the Didache (the Writings of the 12 Apostles), an early writing of the apostles about life in the early church, has to say about kindness. It goes something like this "To insure good treatment of His servants in all ages wherever the gospel might be preached, Jesus made it known that He put a high premium on all acts of kindness done towards them. [1] " What a blessing to read this. What a blessing to

---

1    Bruce, A. B. (1995, c1877). *The training of the twelve or, Passages out of the Gospels, exhibiting the twelve disciples of Jesus under discipline for the apostleship* (113). Oak Harbor, WA: Logos Research Systems, Inc.

know that kindness is one of the gifts of the Holy Spirit for our lives. It always strikes me that teens are great when challenged to perform random acts of kindness. I recently read about a store in one of our major cities that has a small box outside, and as people pass by, it is activated to speak a random act of kindness to the passerby. Try to be like that machine, and just once a day, perform a random act of kindness. It might be something as simple as your helping another student who is having difficulty in a subject in which you excel. Try it and feel the sense of blessing that you have received by that act of kindness.

#37 **Rb** = Rubidium = **R**ighteous **b**eing

THE CALL

To be righteous is to be a person of integrity. Your peers will always respect you because you are a righteous being (person). Rubidium is said to be used for making of special glasses. Yes, special glasses by which to see the world that God has given us. See the world through the glasses of a righteous being. Therefore, to be righteous is to do that which is upright and virtuous. It really means to see and do things differently. Doing them through the glasses of God. The Bible affirms this viewpoint. Read on.

THE WORD OF GOD SAYS...

Psalm 146:8 (RSV)
[8] the LORD opens the eyes of the blind. The LORD lifts up those who are bowed down; the LORD loves the righteous.

Proverbs 10:3,6–7 (RSV)
[3] The LORD does not let the righteous go hungry, but he thwarts the craving of the wicked. . [6] Blessings are on the head of the righteous, but the mouth of the wicked conceals violence. [7] The memory of the righteous is a blessing, but the name of the wicked will rot.

Proverbs 28:1 (RSV)
[1] The wicked flee when no one pursues, but the righteous are bold as a lion.

Proverbs 13:21 (RSV)
[21] Misfortune pursues sinners, but prosperity rewards the righteous.

2 Timothy 4:8 (RSV)
[8] Henceforth there is laid up for me the crown of righteousness, which the Lord, the righteous judge, will award to me on that Day, and not only to me but also to all who have loved his appearing.

Psalm 145:17 (NIV)
[17] The LORD is righteous in all his ways and faithful in all he does.

THE CHALLENGE

It is said that the righteous being is one who will receive from the Lord an incorrupt future life and be in the eternal glory of God. What a reward for one who is that righteous being. What can you as a teen do to be a righteous being. Look through these special glasses at the world, and know that you will not go hungry because you are a righteous being. One way you might consider is doing random acts of kindness for others. Why not try doing something nice for one of your teachers, but do not let them know about it. For example, you could write a note to one of your teachers who have really impressed you. Tell them thanks for helping you, but don't sign it ! When you can do something that exhibits your gifts as a righteous being, you would be so excited that you will make it a point daily to live as a righteousness being.

#55: **Cs** = Cesium = **C**hristian **s**trength

THE CALL

Cesium is not found very often in nature. But it is known to be used in atomic clocks. Perhaps that gives us a great insight into its use, made to provide accuracy for timing instruments. The follower of Christ needs to have an accurate clock for the Lord and to do this requires **C**hristian **s**trength. When you see the code letters for cesium Cs remember to call on your **C**hristian **s**trength to have accuracy in living your life for the Lord.

THE WORD OF GOD SAYS...

Psalm 18:39 (RSV)
[39] For thou didst gird me with strength for the battle; thou didst make my assailants sink under me.

Psalm 28:7 (RSV)
[7] The LORD is my strength and my shield; in him my heart trusts; so I am helped, and my heart exults, and with my song I give thanks to him.

Psalm 46:1 (RSV)
[1] God is our refuge and strength, a very present help in trouble.

Psalm 93:1 (RSV)
[1] The LORD reigns; he is robed in majesty; the LORD is robed, he is girded with strength. Yea, the world is established; it shall never be moved;

Proverbs 24:10 (RSV)
[10] If you faint in the day of adversity, your strength is small.

Sirach 43:30 (RSV)
[30] When you praise the Lord, exalt him as much as you can; for he will surpass even that. When you exalt him, put forth all your strength, and do not grow weary, for you cannot praise him enough.

Isaiah 12:2 (RSV)
[2] "Behold, God is my salvation; I will trust, and will not be afraid; for the LORD GOD is my strength and my song, and he has become my salvation."

1 Timothy 1:12 (RSV)
[12] I thank him who has given me strength for this, Christ Jesus our Lord, because he judged me faithful by appointing me to his service,

1 Corinthians 10:13 (RSV)
[13] No temptation has overtaken you that is not common to man. God is faithful, and he will not let you be tempted beyond your strength, but with the temptation will also provide the way of escape, that you may be able to endure it.

## THE CHALLENGE

The Church needs young people of Christian Strength because they can be the force that helps to pull the Church forward in these times of negativity. The teens of the Church can be the source to provide strength of character to their peers who most often simply are not interested in the Lord or the Church He has founded. Too many teens today want to take the easy way out. They do not want to live with sacrifice or difficulties. But we know that the body will get weak if its muscle fibers are not used and exercised. It is the same with the spiritual nature where it is necessary to have sacrifice and difficulties to strengthen our spiritual fibers. Strength of any kind only grows by exertion. It needs to be precisely timed and a virtue to be attained. Be precise as cesium makes atomic clocks precise. Be precise in your life for the Lord. Try to strengthen your spirit one day this week by taking only five minutes to exercise your mind and memorize one of the scripture quotations above.

#87 **Fr** = Francium = **Fr**iendship

## THE CALL

Francium is another one of those radioactive elements that is extremely rare. Little is known of it and basically it is another one of those mysteries of nature. Francium is the second rarest element on earth. Being rare is a trait of francium, but our spiritual comparative is Friendship. For you a God given friendship is not so rare and indeed is a very special blessing. The words of the Holy Bible give us an insight into what it means to have a friendship and its blessings.

## THE WORD OF GOD SAYS..

Ecclesiastes 4:9–10 (RSV)
⁹ Two are better than one, because they have a good reward for their toil. ¹⁰ For if they fall, one will lift up his fellow; but woe to him who is alone when he falls and has not another to lift him up.

Proverbs 18:24 (RSV)
²⁴ There are friends who pretend to be friends, but there is a friend who sticks closer than a brother.

Sirach 22:20–21 (RSV)
²⁰ One who throws a stone at birds scares them away, and one who reviles a friend will break off the friendship. ²¹ Even if you have drawn your sword against a friend, do not despair, for a renewal of friendship is possible.

Psalm 25:14 (RSV)
¹⁴ The friendship of the LORD is for those who fear him, and he makes known to them his covenant.

John 15:13–15 (RSV)
¹³ Greater love has no man than this, that a man lay down his life for his friends. ¹⁴ You are my friends if you do what I command you. ¹⁵ No longer do I call you servants, for the servant does not know what his master is doing; but I have called you friends, for all that I have heard from my Father I have made known to you.

## THE CHALLENGE

God's word is such a powerful affirmation to what friendship means. Teens seem to know, more than others, how powerful friendships are to them. If you have friends you are not a poor person. One is truly rich if one has friends. If Jesus is your friend what a treasure you have. Teens today in our culture need to be careful not to become isolated. With all of the social media around today many teens are losing the gift of social skills. If you do you will find yourself being frustrated, and even lonely. God created us for friendships. Friendships based on the word of God are solid and not at all superficial or shallow.

The blessing of a true Christian friendship is that it will make your life fulfilling. Since we all need friends in our lives. Pope Benedict XVI had this to say: "A gift of friendship implies a "*yes*" to the friend and a "no" to all that is incompatible with this friendship, to all that is incompatible with the life of God's family, with true life in Christ." (Benedict XVI, 1-8-06 homily)

A true friend helps to make your life fulfilling. Recall your best friend and check it out. Are they not the one you share your victories with? You also know that a friend is one that you can share things with, and they will not be jealous but share happiness with you. They are always there at all times.

"Jesus, of course, does not limit his friendship to certain categories of people: he manifests himself in each and every one of us, and we must see him in everyone and treat him as a friend in everyone, regardless of their situation. But some of our brothers and sisters are in special situations of suffering or need; and Christ wishes to be seen and treated as a friend especially in those people." (John Paul II, homily 2-18-81)

Now is the time for you to do two things. First, thank God for a good friend that you have. Second, celebrate your friendship. Let your friends know you appreciate them as Jesus appreciated His apostles as He called them His friends.

# 2

## JOURNEY THROUGH GROUP TWO, THE AKALINE EARTH METALS AND THE RELATED VIRTUES

The chemical elements of the alkaline earth metals are known as group 2 on the Periodic Chart. The group two elements, and alongside them the spiritual element of virtue, are explored in this chapter.

CHEMICAL ELEMENT:          SPIRITUAL ELEMENT OF
                           VIRTUE:


Number: Name: Symbol

| | | |
|---|---|---|
| 4 Beryllium | Be | **Be**lief |
| 12 Magnesium | Mg | **M**ountain of **G**od |
| 20 Calcium | Ca | **Ca**ring |
| 38 Strontium | Sr | **S**piritual **r**edemption |
| 56 Barium | Ba | **Ba**lance |
| 88 Radium | Ra | **Ra**diate |

#4 **Be** = Beryllium = **Be**lief

THE CALL

Belief is a true jewel of our lives, like the element beryllium, which in its precious state, is known as either aquamarine or emeralds. And you know belief is essential for your eternal salvation. You are called daily to witness to your belief, which is a precious jewel of your life.

THE WORD OF GOD SAYS...

2 Thessalonians 2:13 (RSV)
[13] But we are bound to give thanks to God always for you, brethren beloved by the Lord, because God chose you from the beginning to be saved, through sanctification by the Spirit and belief in the truth.

Psalm 119:66 (RSV)
[66] Teach me good judgment and knowledge, for I believe in thy commandments.

Mark 5:36 (RSV)
[36] But ignoring what they said, Jesus said to the ruler of the synagogue, "Do not fear, only believe."

Mark 16:16 (RSV)
[16] He who believes and is baptized will be saved; but he who does not believe will be condemned.

John 20:31 (RSV)
[31] but these are written that you may believe that Jesus is the

Christ, the Son of God, and that believing you may have life in his name.

John 3:18 (RSV)
[18] He who believes in him is not condemned; he who does not believe is condemned already, because he has not believed in the name of the only Son of God.

John 6:47 (RSV)
[47] Truly, truly, I say to you, he who believes has eternal life.

Mark 9:23 (RSV)
[23] And Jesus said to him, "If you can! All things are possible to him who believes."

THE CHALLENGE

What great promises the Lord gives to you for your belief. In a world of non belief and cynicism and negativity, what a great relief it is to witness to what you believe in your life. Think of the promise the Lord gives "everlasting life"; all "things possible" for the believer; no condemnation. What a gift in a world of negativity. You want those promises and all it requires is your faithfulness to your belief in the Lord Jesus. Belief in other "promises" of the outside world cannot give you those promises. It should be clear the way to choose. Do it and be blessed. Pick a day this week and spend some time talking to the Lord and telling Him you are thankful for your belief in Him. Give up something to prove it. That might be something as simple as not reading your email for a day.

#12 **Mg** = Magnesium = **M**ountain of **G**od

## THE CALL

Have you been to the mountain? You hear it all the time. Go for it! Search for the top of the mountain. Think of those great athletes who are always climbing to reach the heights of the mountain top. Living in Colorado we are blessed with God's beautiful creation of the mountains here. Young people are always climbing the mountains. I am sure that someday there will even be an Olympic sport of mountain climbing. If we go to the Mountain of God we will experience the Magnificent Glory of God.

In nature, magnesium is one of the most plentiful elements in nature. You have probably all had some "fun" with this element. It is the element that ignites upon heating in air and burns with a dazzling white flame. That is the kind of experience it is when you encounter the Lord, you can be a part of the Mountain of God where you rejoice in His Magnificent Glory.

## THE WORD OF GOD SAYS....

Exodus 3:1 (RSV)
¹ Now Moses was keeping the flock of his father-in-law, Jethro, the priest of Midian; and he led his flock to the west side of the wilderness, and came to Horeb, the mountain of God.

Exodus 4:27 (RSV)
²⁷ The LORD said to Aaron, "Go into the wilderness to meet Moses." So he went, and met him at the mountain of God and kissed him.

Micah 4:2 (RSV)

² and many nations shall come, and say: "Come, let us go up to the mountain of the LORD, to the house of the God of Jacob; that he may teach us his ways and we may walk in his paths." For out of Zion shall go forth the law, and the word of the LORD from Jerusalem.

Psalm 48:1 (RSV)

¹ Great is the LORD and greatly to be praised in the city of our God! His holy mountain.

1 Kings 19:4–8 (NIV)

⁴ While he himself went a day's journey into the wilderness. He came to a broom bush, sat down under it and prayed that he might die. "I have had enough, LORD," he said. "Take my life; I am no better than my ancestors." ⁵ Then he lay down under the bush and fell asleep. All at once an angel touched him and said, "Get up and eat." ⁶ He looked around, and there by his head was some bread baked over hot coals, and a jar of water. He ate and drank and then lay down again. ⁷ The angel of the LORD came back a second time and touched him and said, "Get up and eat, for the journey is too much for you." ⁸ So he got up and ate and drank. Strengthened by that food, he traveled forty days and forty nights until he reached Horeb, the mountain of God.

THE CHALLENGE

What a gift God is to us. He wants you to bask in the glory of His mountain. Think of Elijah as he was standing there on the Mountain of God where he had to be overwhelmed with an incredible experience as he spoke with the Lord and witnessed His magnificent wonders. God wants you to lift your eyes to the heavens and proclaim that He is Lord. His word tells us to shout it from the mountain top. What does that mean to teens today? It means that you have to know in your heart that God is for you. Know in your heart that God wants to ignite in you with a dazzling white flame, just as Magnesium does in nature. Let it go forth from you. That is how you shout it from the Mountain of God. Now take it to heart and be a dazzling example of goodness that God has blessed you with. Do not fear, as Elijah did not fear, to be a good person and reflect that goodness with confidence to your peers.

#20 **Ca** = Calcium = **Ca**ring

## THE CALL

You have such beautiful teeth! Are your bones strong? If your response is yes, then you know biologically how important calcium is for you. Without it you would not have those beautiful teeth or strong bones. Just as calcium gives you an important set of strengths in life, so does Caring do for you in the realm of the Lord. An attitude of caring gives you strength of character and ads integrity to your personality.

## THE WORD OF GOD SAYS...

I Timothy 5:4 (NIV)
⁴ But if a widow has children or grandchildren, these should learn first of all to put their religion into practice by caring for their own family and so repaying their parents and grandparents, for this is pleasing to God.

Luke 10:35 (RSV)
[35] And the next day he took out two denarii and gave them to the innkeeper, saying, 'Take care of him; and whatever more you spend, I will repay you when I come back.'

Psalm 8:4 (RSV)
[4] what is man that thou art mindful of him, and the son of man that thou dost care for him?

Hebrews 2:6 (RSV)
[6] It has been testified somewhere, "What is man that thou art mindful of him, or the son of man, that thou carest for him?

1 Peter 5:7 (RSV)
[7] Cast all your anxieties on him, for he cares about you.

Psalm 146:5–9 (RSV)
[5] Happy is he whose help is the God of Jacob, whose hope is in the LORD his God, [6] who made heaven and earth, the sea, and all that is in them; who keeps faith for ever; [7] who executes justice for the oppressed; who gives food to the hungry.
The LORD sets the prisoners free; [8] the LORD opens the eyes of the blind. The LORD lifts up those who are bowed down; the LORD loves the righteous. [9] The LORD watches over the sojourners, he upholds the widow and the fatherless; but the way of the wicked he brings to ruin.

THE CHALLENGE

Many teens are known for their acts of caring. I know of a parish where one of the service projects they have is to help build houses for the poor with Habitat for Humanity. It is also a reality that many teens just do not care to be involved in anything but themselves. Yet when we look at what makes a person strong they need to have a solid skeleton, like the body, with solid bones to help them stand up for what the Lord teaches. In Psalm 146 we hear of several ways in which God cares for His people. These are the basics of what we call the corporal works of mercy (To feed the hungry. To give drink to the thirsty. To clothe the naked. To visit and ransom the captives. To shelter the homeless. To visit the sick. To bury the dead. ). All of these are CARING moments. Therefore, it is time to understand that some of the most basic works of mercy would be involved in communication and caring. It takes some sacrifice on your part to be that CARING person. Think right now of one of the corporal works of mercy you could do in your community. Settle on it, and then try to translate a variation of this for another teen. What a way to give witness to putting into action the CARING attitude that Christ expects of you.

#38: **Sr** = Strontium = **S**piritual **r**edemption

THE CALL

The meaning of spiritual redemption for me is the end effect of what happens to us in the future. Saint John Paul II said in his Theology of the Body, that "In the resurrection the human body, according to the words of the Apostle, is seen "incorruptible, glorious, full of dynamism, spiritual.""

You have seen strontium at work and may not have known it. Recall the last celebration of the 4th of July when you saw fireworks. Remember those red colors in the fireworks display? That was strontium. You may have also seen it in the red flares used at the time of an accident when the police put out flares to direct traffic. Fireworks all go up, and tradition teaches us that heaven is up. Just as Jesus ascended, that is, He went up. Therefore, this is what our spiritual redemption will achieve, our going to heaven to receive the gifts that Saint John Paul II spoke of.

## THE WORD OF GOD SAYS...

### Romans 5:10–11 (NIV)

[10] For if, while we were God's enemies, we were reconciled to him through the death of his Son, how much more, having been reconciled, shall we be saved through his life! [11] Not only is this so, but we also boast in God through our Lord Jesus Christ, through whom we have now received reconciliation.

### Romans 8:23 (RSV)

[23] and not only the creation, but we ourselves, who have the first fruits of the Spirit, groan inwardly as we wait for adoption as sons, the redemption of our bodies.

### 1 Corinthians 15:49 (RSV)

[49] Just as we have borne the image of the man of dust, we shall also bear the image of the man of heaven.

### Ephesians 1:3–7 (RSV)

[3] Blessed be the God and Father of our Lord Jesus Christ, who has blessed us in Christ with every spiritual blessing in the heavenly places, [4] even as he chose us in him before the foundation of the world, that we should be holy and blameless before him. [5] He destined us in love to be his sons through Jesus Christ, according to the purpose of his will, [6] to the praise of his glorious

grace which he freely bestowed on us in the Beloved. [7] In him we have redemption through his blood, the forgiveness of our trespasses, according to the riches of his grace

## THE CHALLENGE

It is not often that a teen thinks about dying and going to heaven. It is not often that a teen thinks of fear either. But both of these are realities and can happen at any time. During my time of teaching high school biology, it was always a sad moment for us when one of the students was killed. No one thought that it would ever happen, but it did. It is important for you to think about this possibility. It is therefore, important to see that our spiritual redemption is taken care of. You do this by a good faithful living of what God wants you to do. Living a good moral life and making all the right choices. It really is keeping the commandments. This will keep you on the path to holiness which will lead to your spiritual redemption, your flaring up to heaven one day. Spend some time one day just thinking about going to heaven. Then say to yourself that you really do want to be holy.

## #56 **Ba**rium = Ba = **Ba**lance

## THE CALL:

Sometimes a doctor will want to examine the outlines of your internal organs and will give you a barium swallow to take x-rays to show up that outline. While this may be uncomfortable, it provides an interesting way to solve health problems. But this can only be done with barium which provides a balanced environment for this analysis. Balance is also a virtue that is necessary in the life of faith because it provides the outline of our faith and helps to show up any non-balanced things in your life of faith.

## THE WORD OF GOD SAYS...

Job 31:6 (RSV)
[6] Let me be weighed in a just balance, and let God know my integrity!

Proverbs 11:1 (RSV)
[1] A false balance is an abomination to the LORD, but a just weight is his delight.

Proverbs 16:11 (RSV)
[11] A just balance and scales are the LORD's; all the weights in the bag are his work.

Sirach 21:25 (RSV)
[25] The lips of strangers will speak of these things, but the words of the prudent will be weighed in the balance.

Psalm 62:9 (NIV84)
[9] Lowborn men are but a breath, the highborn are but a lie; if weighed on a balance, they are nothing; together they are only a breath.

## THE CHALLENGE:

The Word of God above tells us that "false balance is an abomination to the Lord".

Thus you need always to be sure that you have balance in your faith. St. Thomas Aquinas always said that in the middle (balanced position) is where strength lies. If you have strength of faith then have that balance. Why is it so necessary? Balance in life is important to make good moral choices. It might be compared to a strong spice, too much pepper, for example. Put too much pepper on your food and you cannot control the results, and you are therefore, not balanced. Another way to think of balance is that you center your life in Christ. A crooked picture hanging off balance looks pretty weird. So too does a life that is not balanced in Christ. Ask yourself today if there is any area of your life that is out of balance with what Christ expects of you. Did you violate one of His commandments? For example, have you spent too much time playing video games, time on the internet, or texting and not doing your homework? Then you need to seek His forgiveness immediately. Then you are back in balance and we will see the clear outlines of who you really are.

#88 **Ra** = Radium = **Ra**diate

THE CALL

You have all heard of radium in your science classes. You also know that radium is radioactive and it radiates. Radium is said to be in naturally present in the environment in very small amounts. Being naturally present means, we are therefore exposed to this element. We do not need radium, but, if it is present, it radiates. This has a spiritual connection for us. We need to radiate in our environment because of the presence of the Holy Trinity in each of us. We might best understand what it means to radiate if we think of a light bulb. When it is energized, it radiates, that is, gives off light its energy. Thinking of light and how it radiates, read God's word to see how God speaks to us of that radiating gift.

## THE WORD OF GOD OF GOD SAYS...

### Matthew 5:14–16 (RSV)
[14] "You are the light of the world. A city set on a hill cannot be hid. [15] Nor do men light a lamp and put it under a bushel, but on a stand, and it gives light to all in the house. [16] Let your light so shine before men, that they may see your good works and give glory to your Father who is in heaven.

### 1 Peter 2:9 (RSV)
[9] But you are a chosen race, a royal priesthood, a holy nation, God's own people, that you may declare the wonderful deeds of him who called you out of darkness into his marvelous light.

### Hebrews 1:3 (RSV)
[3] He reflects the glory of God and bears the very stamp of his nature, upholding the universe by his word of power. When he had made purification for sins, he sat down at the right hand of the Majesty on high.

### Matthew 17:2 (RSV)
[2] And he was transfigured before them, and his face shone like the sun, and his garments became white as light.

### Mark 9:3 (RSV)
[3] and his garments became glistening, intensely white, as no fuller on earth could bleach them.

2 Corinthians 4:4 (RSV)
<sup>4</sup> In their case the god of this world has blinded the minds of the unbelievers, to keep them from seeing the light of the gospel of the glory of Christ, who is the likeness of God.

## THE CHALLENGE

You can easily see from God's word, that as Jesus radiates the Father to us, we need to radiate Jesus to our world. The question for teens today is an important one. The question for you: Is the light of Christ shining through you? Is that light shining to your family and friends?

Remember they are observing you, watching you and what you do. Is your life an example that you will radiate Jesus? Living your faith is your testimony. The challenge for you then is to make each day a day that radiates the light of faith to others. It is a kind of spiritual osmosis, that your faith is oozing out from you all the time. The result is that you will radiate Jesus and be a light to others. This is the work of saints and you are called to be one.

When you radiate for the Lord in doing good deeds it will always give glory to God. How well you radiate Jesus will benefit others. This will bring others to whom you radiate to God.

While working with teens in youth ministry I was always impressed by a song by Toby Mac called "In The Light." Read the lyrics below, reflect on them and then ask the big question, "how does this apply to me?" Or "how does this message help you radiate the light of Christ?" Enjoy, here are the lyrics of that song.

# PERIODIC CHART OF VIRTUOUS LIVING FOR TEENS

I keep trying to find a life
On my own, apart from you
I am the king of excuses
I've got one for every selfish thing I do

What's going on inside of me?
I despise my own behavior
This only serves to confirm my suspicions
That I'm still a man in need of a saviour

I wanna be in the Light
As You are in the Light
I wanna shine like the stars in the heavens
Oh, Lord be my Light and be my salvation
'Cause all I want is to be in the Light
All I want is to be in the Light

The disease of self runs through my blood
It's a cancer fatal to my soul
Every attempt on my behalf has failed
To bring this sickness under control

I wanna be in the Light
As You are in the Light
I wanna shine like the stars in the heavens
Oh, Lord be my Light and be my salvation
'Cause all I want is to be in the Light
All I want is to be in the Light

Honesty becomes me (There's nothing left to lose)
The secrets that did run me (In Your Presence are defused)
Pride has no position (And riches have no worth)
The fame that once did cover me (Has been sentenced to this
earth)
Has been sentenced to this earth

# 3

## THE JOURNEY THROUGH THE ELEMENTS AND VIRTUES OF THE TRANSITION METALS IN GROUPS 3, 4 AND SELECTED LANTHANIDES OF 4F

In this chapter we will consider those elements known as transition metals of groups 3 and 4. Then we expand the consideration of the "off the chart" elements known as the Lanthanides in group 4f. We only treat of a limited number of elements in group 4f.

As is our pattern we will establish the virtues related to the symbols of these elements.

These are the elements and virtues we will consider in this chapter.

CHEMICAL ELEMENT:    SPIRITUAL ELEMENT OF
                     VIRTUE:

Number: Name: Symbol

GROUP 3:

| | | |
|---|---|---|
| 21 Scandium | Sc | **Sc**holars for the Lord |
| 39 Yttrium | Y | **Y**ield to the Lord |

GROUP 4:

| | | |
|---|---|---|
| 22 Titanium | Ti | **Ti**thing |
| 40 Zirconium | Zr | **Z**eal **r**eborn |
| 72 Hafnium | Hf | **H**oly **F**amily |

LANTHANIDES GROUP 4f

| | | |
|---|---|---|
| 57 Lanthanum | La | **La**ughter |
| 58 Cerium | Ce | **Ce**lebrate |
| 59 Praseodymium | Pr | **Pr**udence |
| 60 Neodymium | Nd | **N**on-**d**estructive |
| 61 Promethium | Pm | **P**ro-**m**agnanimous |
| 62 Samarium | Sm | **Sm**ile |

GROUP 3:

#21: **Sc** = Scandium = **Sc**holars for the Lord

THE CALL

The function of scholars is to bring light and understanding to others. They spend their time in study and then share their efforts with others. You are all students and you the recipients of the work of all kinds of scholars. I know that the scholars

I remember most, when I was a student, were the ones who made me reach for a higher good. They often pushed me to do more. Scandium is not well known in our culture, but it does have some functions that help to shed "light" on the role of scholars too. Scandium, as a compound known as an iodide, when added to mercury vapor lamps, produces a highly efficient light source resembling sunlight, which is important for indoor or night-time color TV transmission. Seek out those scholars who push you to shine brightly.

## THE WORD OF GOD SAYS...

1 Corinthians 1:20 (RSV)
[20] Where is the wise man? Where is the scribe? Where is the debater of this age? Has not God made foolish the wisdom of the world?

John 7:15 (RSV)
[15] The Jews marveled at it, saying, "How is it that this man has learning, when he has never studied?"

Acts 18:24 (RSV)
[24] Now a Jew named Apollos, a native of Alexandria, came to Ephesus. He was an eloquent man, well versed in the scriptures.

Luke 10:37 (RSV)
[37] He said, "The one who showed mercy on him." And Jesus said to him, "Go and do likewise."

Luke 10:25 (RSV)
[25] And behold, a lawyer stood up to put him to the test, saying, "Teacher, what shall I do to inherit eternal life?"

## THE CHALLENGE

To be a scholar for the Lord is to be one interested in the truth. This requires that we appreciate the scriptures when they tell us "to know God is to love God." To have that knowledge requires that we are willing to spend time to be a scholar of God's word. When we understand the strength of God's word, we find that its Divine origin is the source for authority in our lives. To be a scholar of the Lord and accept the Lord's authority over you is what makes you a person of character. The Church has been blessed with holy scholars. We call the most notable of them Doctors of the Church. Take time to search on your computer for Doctors of the Church and then try reading just a little of their writings and see their wisdom. You will be amazed at how their words have a practical application to you in your world today. Hint: try reading some of the writings of St. Thomas Aquinas.

#39: **Y** = Yttrium = **Y**ield to the Lord

## THE CALL

Who ever heard of Yttrium? Only if you work with lasers would you know what it is Lasers are one of its uses. But you have heard of Yield. You have seen the street sign that says "yield." A great image for you is to do what God wants you to do. That is to yield to Him. Think of that yield sign that you see at many intersections. Then you have some idea of what it means for you in your spiritual journey. Yield to God, do His will and you will have eternal life.

## THE WORD OF GOD SAYS...

**2 Chronicles 30:8 (RSV)**
[8] Do not now be stiff-necked as your fathers were, but yield yourselves to the LORD, and come to his sanctuary, which he has sanctified forever, and serve the LORD your God, that his fierce anger may turn away from you.

**Joshua 24:23 (NIV)**
[23] "Now then," said Joshua, "throw away the foreign gods that are among you and yield your hearts to the LORD, the God of Israel."

**Romans 6:13 (RSV)**
[13] Do not yield your members to sin as instruments of wickedness, but yield yourselves to God as men who have been brought from death to life, and your members to God as instruments of righteousness.

**Psalm 141:4 (NAB)**
[4] Do not let my heart incline to evil, or yield to any sin.
I will never feast upon the fine food of evildoers.

## THE CHALLENGE

To Yield to the Lord is not easy, especially for a teen. But without it you cannot really learn to grow in holiness. Think of the situation when you go to Mass. Do you really enter into the praise and worship? Some of the women will, but many of the men will hold back, that is they are not yielding. If you do not yield you will not experience the power of the Holy Spirit in your life. And if you do not yield and have this experience you are missing an incredible freedom to be a son and daughter of the Lord. But if you do, you will penetrate our world with incredible precision, just as a laser penetrates with ultimate precision. Yielding is letting yourself go to do the work God wants you to do. Try to yield to the promptings of the Lord this week. When you go to Mass this Sunday, really be a part of the time of worship. Open yourself to the Holy Spirit and let him fill you with His light. Doing this you will be one who experiences the power of the Holy Spirit to give you a new feeling of being blessed. Celebrate your peacefulness of heart and join in the singing. Experience what St. Augustine told us that to "sing well is to pray twice."

GROUP 4:

#22: **Ti** = Titanium = **Ti**thing

THE CALL

The bible gives us many clear indications of the blessings of one who tithes. Tithing is giving one's first resourses for the work of the Church. In the Bible it often speaks of the tithe as ten percent. The essence of tithing is giving back to the Lord the first part of all of your resources, and not just what is left over. This is not an interesting virtue of life for the typical teen. But think of it like the element titanium which is light weight and strong. It gives its all, if you will, its nature, is to do what it was created for. That is like giving its first fruits to its work in nature. You are called to do no less for the Lord.

## THE WORD OF GOD SAYS...

Deuteronomy 14:22 (RSV)
[22] "You shall tithe all the yield of your seed, which comes forth from the field year by year.

Sirach 35:7–9 (RSV)
[7] The sacrifice of a righteous man is acceptable, and the memory of it will not be forgotten. [8] Glorify the Lord generously, and do not stint the first fruits of your hands. [9] With every gift show a cheerful face, and dedicate your tithe with gladness.

Nehemiah 10:38 (RSV)
[38] And the priest, the son of Aaron, shall be with the Levites when the Levites receive the tithes; and the Levites shall bring up the tithe of the tithes to the house of our God, to the chambers, to the storehouse.

Luke 18:10–12 (RSV)
[10] "Two men went up into the temple to pray, one a Pharisee and the other a tax collector. [11] The Pharisee stood and prayed thus with himself, 'God, I thank thee that I am not like other men, extortioners, unjust, adulterers, or even like this tax collector. [12] I fast twice a week, I give tithes of all that I get.'

## THE CHALLENGE

In 1848 John P. Rockefeller Sr. gave this testimony. "Yes, I tithe, and I would like to tell you how it all came about. I had to begin work as a small boy to help support my mother. My first wages amounted to $1.50 per week. The first week after I went to work, I took the $1.50 home to my mother and she held the money in her lap and explained to me that she would be happy if I would give a tenth of it to the Lord.

I did, and from that week until this day I have tithed every dollar God has entrusted to me. And I want to say, if I had not tithed the first dollar I made I would not have tithed the first million dollars I made. Tell your readers to train the children to tithe, and they will grow up to be faithful stewards of the Lord.
—John P. Rockefeller, Sr."[2]

Rockefeller was one of the wealthiest men in the world. But it has also been said that the best tithers are the ones that start who are poor (e.g.: Someone says that tithing is only for the rich. But we have never heard of a rich man or woman commencing tithing, but can name scores who began to tithe when they were poor and became rich:

Mr. Crowell, founder of Quaker Oats Co.
Mr. Colgate, founder of Colgate Soaps, etc.
Mr. Proctor of Ivory soap fame
Mr. A. A. Hyde of Mentholatum
Mr. Henry Delaney of Resinol Ointment fame
Mr. Matthias Baldwin, founder of Baldwin Locomotive Industry.

What a witness I have experienced seeing teens who are open to tithing. The teen who gives 10% of the weekly allowance will not be a selfish person. The employed teen who gives that first 10%, of the meager enough weekly check, to the work of

---

2    Tan, P. L. (1996, c1979). *Encyclopedia of 7700 illustrations* , Garland TX: Bible Communications.

the Lord in a tithe at the time of the offering at Mass is a true witness. It is a way of life. It is a recognition of the sovereignty of God over all things. Think of it this way. When you give the first 10% to the Lord, He still leaves you with 90% for your own use. There is more than enough there. Think of starting it. Why not start a plan of tithing. Go toward tithing, start the first month giving 2% of your resources, then the next month increase that by another 2% until you reach the minimum of 10% and you will see how it makes you feel. You will have a sense of really participating in the work of your parish.

#40 **Zr** = Zirconium = **Z**eal **r**eborn

## THE CALL

Zirconium is known to have great properties of refraction. This means it sends back to you a certain brightness. It is because of this property of refraction that zirconium is used in gems. Think of something that refracts and looks precious. In God's world this is exactly what zeal means. You have such excitement (zeal) that you are energizing, or giving life to others. This excitement should become infective so that it spreads to many other young people from you.

## THE WORD OF GOD SAYS...

Isaiah 26:11 (RSV)
[11] O LORD, thy hand is lifted up, but they see it not. Let them see thy zeal for thy people, and be ashamed. Let the fire for thy adversaries consume them.

Psalm 69:9 (RSV)
⁹ For zeal for thy house has consumed me, and the insults of those who insult thee have fallen on me.

John 2:17 (RSV)
¹⁷ His disciples remembered that it was written, "Zeal for thy house will consume me."

Romans 12:11 (RSV)
¹¹ Never flag in zeal, be aglow with the Spirit, serve the Lord.

2 Corinthians 7:12 (RSV)
¹² So although I wrote to you, it was not on account of the one who did the wrong, nor on account of the one who suffered the wrong, but in order that your zeal for us might be revealed to you in the sight of God.

THE CHALLENGE

How does a teen have this zeal of the scriptures? I believe that if you have 3 E's for your life, you will have that apostolic zeal reborn. The three E's are: energy, excitement, and enthusiasm. In everything you do, have these three qualities and everyone around you will experience your zeal for the Lord. Remember zeal is excitement for God. If your zeal is filled with the spirit of Jesus and is inspired with your obedience and love for the Church, it will be tremendous in blessing others who know you. Be an agent to carry the truths of the Church to other teens. The Church needs you to do this to preserve a sense of goodness in future generations. You can see that the Church sets a high bar for you. You are essential to growth of the Church. Remember you must reflect the truths of the Church like a precious jewel. Do not keep the beauty of the truths of our faith to yourself, but reflect it to your peers and others around you. When Lent comes around again in the calendar why not make it one of the things that you will do each day of Lent. The doing of the 3 E's with your faith can exert an incredible influence among your peers and in your family. Do something each day of Lent to demonstrate your zeal to grow the Church. All it takes is for you to be a person of action for the Church. Follow what I like to call "Nike theology", JUST DO IT!

#72 = **Hf** = Hafnium = **H**oly **f**amily

THE CALL

The element Hafnium is a lustrous silver color in nature and is able to resist corrosion and does not melt except under extreme conditions. These are interesting qualities as we use this element of remind us of the Holy Family. You already know that the Holy Family , Jesus, Mary and Joseph, were a very lustrous family in the Holy Land. We also know that under extreme conditions they did "not melt". Take that to mean that they did not bend from their values given them by God.

THE WORD

Sirach 3:2–7 (RSV)
² For the Lord honored the father above the children, and he confirmed the right of the mother over her sons. ³ Whoever honors his father atones for sins, ⁴ and whoever glorifies his mother is like one who lays up treasure. ⁵ Whoever honors his father will be gladdened by his own children, and when he prays he will be heard. ⁶ Whoever glorifies his father will have

long life, and whoever obeys the Lord will refresh his mother; [7] he will serve his parents as his masters.

Matthew 2:13–15 (RSV)

[13] Now when they had departed, behold, an angel of the Lord appeared to Joseph in a dream and said, "Rise, take the child and his mother, and flee to Egypt, and remain there till I tell you; for Herod is about to search for the child, to destroy him." [14] And he rose and took the child and his mother by night, and departed to Egypt, [15] and remained there until the death of Herod. This was to fulfill what the Lord had spoken by the prophet, "Out of Egypt have I called my son."

## THE CHALLENGE

We get a great perspective of the Holy Family and their ability "not to melt" from a prayer given by Saint John Paul II on the feast of the Holy Family. He said: "May the Holy Family, who had to overcome many painful trials, watch over all the families in the world, especially those who are experiencing difficult situations. May the Holy Family also help men and women of culture and political leaders so that they may defend the institution of the family, based on marriage, and so that they may sustain the family as it confronts the grave challenges of the modern age!"

What an encouragement God's word gives to the concept of holy families with the example of THE HOLY FAMILY. God's word also gives us many insights into the behavior that all members of a family should have. The words from the book of Sirach are incredible in that there is a duty for each member of the family to do their part. In these words there is a challenge to each member to do all that you can to develop harmony and peace in the family. What a joy it would be for you as sons and daughters of your families to give joy to your parents by your obedience and love. You could not do more than that to develop harmony in your families. This week think of one thing that you could do for your mother and one thing for your father that they would not normally expect from you. For example, why not just help with dishes, or taking out the trash, or washing the car without being asked. You will be rewarded for that random act of kindness to your parents by God. Do not look for them necessarily to say something to you, but know that the Lord sees it and blesses it. That is your blessing and you need nothing more. I believe that this will be a great trust builder for sons or daughters by their parents. It will prove that you will not melt to the extreme demands in society to just "do your own thing."

## LANTHANIDES GROUP 4f

#57: **La** = Lanthanum = **La**ughter

THE CALL:

Lanthanum has some modern day uses for example in batteries that are used in the new hybrid automobiles. Most notably it's compounds are used in carbon lighting applications that you would find in TV studio lighting. When it is combined with oxygen, as an oxide of lanthanum, the compound can be used to make camera and telescope lenses. How interesting this element is in nature. Just think about it, batteries to give power and in studio lighting to brighten the set for broadcast. These are qualities every follower of the Lord should also have, power and light of life of the Lord in them. Ever think of being in a dark room and there is no light? Is it possible to think that a person who can add a moment of laughter might bring a moment of light to that situation. A great way to provide light into another's life is the blessed power of laughter, that will brighten any darkness.

THE WORD:

Job 8:21 (RSV)
²¹ He will yet fill your mouth with laughter, and your lips with shouting.

Psalm 126:2 (RSV)
² Then our mouth was filled with laughter, and our tongue with shouts of joy; then they said among the nations, "The LORD has done great things for them."

James 4:9 (RSV)
⁹ Be wretched and mourn and weep. Let your laughter be turned to mourning and your joy to dejection.

Sirach 19:29–30 (RSV)
²⁹ A man is known by his appearance, and a sensible man is known by his face, when you meet him. ³⁰ A man's attire and open-mouthed laughter, and a man's manner of walking, show what he is.

THE CHALLENGE:

God's word tells us that laughter shows who a person is. Think of this, if you combined your laughter, and it has the effect of the natural element lanthanum (power and light), you can do powerful things for God in our world that has lost all of its power because it has lost its sense of direction of doing good and avoiding evil. With this lack of direction there is little laughter, and so there is little light in many people's lives. You can do so much to bring the laughter of the Lord into our world and as the Psalm tells us "the Lord has done great things for us."

He wants us to be a joyful people. Therefore, your present challenge is to try to bring a moment of laughter into someone's life this week. Think of what you can do to get someone to smile, and then affirm them in the Lord, for their smile. Not only will you do something that makes them feel blessed but you will also be blessed because of your random act of kindness to one of God's creatures.

#58 = **Ce** = Cerium = **Ce**lebrate

THE CALL

Cerium is another of those elements that you do not find often or hear of often, but you experience it in ways unknown to you. Several of its compounds such as oxide of cerium are used in very familiar ways by you. For example cerium oxide is found in the catalytic converter of your car. Your mom probably is not aware that it is found in the walls of her self-cleaning oven. I bet she celebrates when she does not have to do the scrubbing of the oven to clean it, thanks to cerium oxide. Have you ever been in a school drama production and the lighting crew used a follow spot? Well the carbon-arc bulb used in that instrument uses cerium oxide. Bet you celebrated when the follow spot was on you! Again, things that bring joy to one's life are reasons to celebrate.

## THE WORD OF GOD SAYS...

1 Corinthians 5:8 (RSV)
[8] Let us, therefore, celebrate the festival, not with the old leaven, the leaven of malice and evil, but with the unleavened bread of sincerity and truth.

Luke 15:24 (ESV)
[24] For this my son was dead, and is alive again; he was lost, and is found.' And they began to celebrate.

3 Maccabees 6:33 (RSV)
[33] Likewise also the king, after convening a great banquet to celebrate these events, gave thanks to heaven unceasingly and lavishly for the unexpected rescue which he had experienced.

Exodus 12:14 (NIV)
[14] "This is a day you are to commemorate; for the generations to come you shall celebrate it as a festival to the LORD—a lasting ordinance.

Psalm 145:7 (NIV)
[7] They celebrate your abundant goodness and joyfully sing of your righteousness.

Matthew 26:18 (NIV)
[18] He replied, "Go into the city to a certain man and tell him, 'The Teacher says: My appointed time is near. I am going to celebrate the Passover with my disciples at your house.' "

## THE CHALLENGE

You want to celebrate the Lord in your life. There is a daily blessing in your life and that is that you have life. Yes, you should celebrate each day that the Lord gives you, to be alive in His kingdom on earth. Just think about it as another day to prepare you for the great gift of Heaven. One of the great ways you can celebrate the gift of life each day is to try to attend Mass more than just on Sunday. Maybe you can also celebrate this great gift by going to adoration once or twice a week. Let the Lord's follow-spot be on you each day as you give thanks. You do have time to do this and it will not ruin your day or your schedule. Actually it will even make your day more enjoyable. Therefore, sometime this week, celebrate the gift of life God has given you by going to adoration or at least pay a visit to the chapel in your school or parish church. You will feel that you have been cleansed, just like the walls of an oven with God's special presence within you.

#59 = **Pr** = Praseodymium = **Pr**udence

## THE CALL

If you ever had those yellow lens on your sunglasses or ski glasses it has praseodymium in it. Notice that this kind of glass acts as a filter. Also notice that Prudence acts as a filter for many of our actions. You will recall that Prudence is one of the cardinal virtues of our faith. Read now how we are taught by God's word about prudence.

## THE WORD OF GOD SAYS...

Proverbs 1:2-5 (RSV)
[2] That men may know wisdom and instruction, understand words of insight, [3] receive instruction in wise dealing, righteousness, justice, and equity; [4] that prudence may be given to the simple, knowledge and discretion to the youth— [5] the wise man also may hear and increase in learning, and the man of understanding acquire skill,

Proverbs 8:5 (RSV)
[5] O simple ones, learn prudence; O foolish men, pay attention.

Proverbs 19:25 (RSV)
[25] Strike a scoffer, and the simple will learn prudence; reprove a man of understanding, and he will gain knowledge.

Sirach 19:22 (RSV)
[22] But the knowledge of wickedness is not wisdom, nor is there prudence where sinners take counsel.

Sirach 22:27 (RSV)
[27] O that a guard were set over my mouth, and a seal of prudence upon my lips, that it may keep me from falling, so that my tongue may not destroy me!

Proverbs 15:5 (NIV)
[5] A fool spurns his father's discipline, but whoever heeds correction shows prudence

## THE CHALLENGE

The Catechism of the Catholic Church teaches that: "Prudence is 'right reason in action,' writes St. Thomas Aquinas. It is called the charioteer of the virtues; it guides the other virtues by setting rule and measure. It is prudence that immediately guides the judgment of conscience. The prudent man determines and directs his conduct in accordance with this judgment. With the help of this virtue we apply moral principles to particular cases without error and overcome doubts about the good to achieve and the evil to avoid." (CCC # 1806)

Young people should consider that Prudence is a most needed of the cardinal virtues for their life. You need to develop this great gift from the Lord so that all ages of people will have a deeper belief in you. This shows that you are maturing and can use your mind to think before you act. What a great witness this will be to a world, and especially other young people, who just act so often without thinking of the consequences of a decision. When you are prudent you learn to balance and consider all of the circumstances about a decision. If you do not, then others will say you are inconsistent and not thinking. Do not let this be a description of who you are as a person. After you make your next decision, not matter what it is, ask yourself this question, "was that a prudent decision, did I filter what was necessary to make it a moral decision." If the answer is yes, then you have advanced on the road to holiness. Congratulations!

#60 = **Nd** = Neodymium = **N**on-**d**estructive

## THE CALL

A non-destructive person is one who does the contrary for others. If you are non-destructive then you are one who builds up. Building up others is a great virtue for a teen, especially with peers who are not accepted in some of your classes. Neodymium (Nd) is generally combined with other substances to build up what it can do. When an element is combined with another we say that it is an alloy. If you combine neodymium with iron and boron you make great magnets. These powerful magnets are used in your computer data storage devices or, if you have some great speakers with your audio system in your room its magnets have this alloy. Even in nature this element is used to build up its effect by joining with other elements. Living God's life expects us to work with others to build them up. The Bible has some interesting insights for you.

## THE WORD OF GOD SAYS:

Isaiah 57:14 (RSV)
[14] And it shall be said, "Build up, build up, prepare the way, remove every obstruction from my people's way."

Ecclesiastes 3:3 (RSV)
[3] a time to kill, and a time to heal; a time to break down, and a time to build up;

Psalm 28:5 (RSV)
[5] Because they do not regard the works of the LORD, or the work of his hands, he will break them down and build them up no more.

Acts 20:32 (RSV)
³² And now I commend you to God and to the word of his grace, which is able to build you up and to give you the inheritance among all those who are sanctified.

1 Thessalonians 5:11 (RSV)
¹¹ Therefore encourage one another and build one another up, just as you are doing.

Jude 20 (RSV)
²⁰ But you, beloved, build yourselves up on your most holy faith; pray in the Holy Spirit.

## THE CHALLENGE

Building up your brothers and sisters, your classmates, your friends makes you a magnet for the Lord. Building up others is a great virtue for a teen, especially with peers who are not accepted in some of your classes. Maybe you are very good at biology and another students is not. Build up that person and help them learn rather than let them destroy themselves in the class. This will be a great testimony to you that you are a mature follower of Jesus. He needs you to do this effort, of building up, so that others can also grow as members of the Body of Christ that St. Paul always talks about. Remember each person has been given gifts. When you build up another person you affirm them and recognize that God has given them gifts that are different than the one's he has given you. Be a builder for the Lord.

#61 = **Pm** = Promethium = **P**ro **m**agnanimous

THE CALL

Want a twenty-five cent word, look at promagnanimous for starters. It has a profound definition. It means to be one who is known for being a lofty and noble person of generous spirit. That is truly a virtue the Lord would find helpful in teens today. A person of generous spirit or heart is one who radiates a very positive attitude to others. Promethium is very radioactive and rare in nature. While this element is often used in pacemakers and a light source for signals it is still rare. It is rare as a person with a pro magnanimous personality.

Examine what the Bible teaches on such a person.

THE WORD OF GOD SAYS...

Psalm 16:3 (RSV)
³ As for the saints in the land, they are the noble, in whom is all my delight.

Proverbs 8:6 (RSV)
⁶ Hear, for I will speak noble things, and from my lips will come what is right;

Isaiah 32:8 (RSV)
⁸ But he who is noble devises noble things, and by noble things he stands.

Romans 12:17 (RSV)
[17] Repay no one evil for evil, but take thought for what is noble in the sight of all.

2 Timothy 2:21 (RSV)
[21] If any one purifies himself from what is ignoble, then he will be a vessel for noble use, consecrated and useful to the master of the house, ready for any good work.

## THE CHALLENGE

You have probably met a person that is a pro-magnanimous individual. They are those people whom you have met who change who you are. Anything can effect a change in you. Do you have an unusual feeling when you hear a special piece of music? Some teens are greatly affected by certain movies. You may have had a dramatic change because of the special help you got from a teacher who was really special and reached out to you. It may have been a coach that really developed your potential. These are pro-magnanimous individuals they are the ones who make a noble effort for you. They have that generous spirit that really excites you and gives you great dreams for your future. They give you special signals to develop your gifts. Jesus is the same for us. He has that most generous spirit and is always willing to give us His help (grace) that we can develop our gifts for use in His Church. The Lord is the greatest pro-magnanimous person in the world. He is not a jealous God. He is a generous God and is always giving to us. Show your generosity for all that He has given you. Think one day this week of one of your gifts that has grown since you began high school. Then give thanks to God for that gift and at the same time ask the Lord to continue to grow the gift in you. Remember that a person who is pro-magnanimous is living this virtue and aims to do great things for God. God did it, now it is your turn to do it. To be a pro magnanimous person is to be one who aspires to holiness. That kind of person aims to do great things for God. Be a P.M. (pro-magnanimous) person.

#62 = **Sm** = Samarium = **Sm**ile

THE CALL

Samarium is not a common everyday word and it is not a common everyday element. It is known as one of the rare elements and the fifth most abundant of the rare elements.

Even though it is found in the United States we do not see it on jars of peanut butter. The reason is that it has no biological functions. In chemical reactions it is used as a catalyst especially to hydrate ethanol. Many of you use ethanol during the winter in your car gasoline. It is difficult to draw a connection to nature for us, but the symbol of this element is Sm which can stand for us to SMile. A person who smiles is always a gracious person who is delighted with little. They live a happy attitude.

THE WORD OF GOD SAYS...

Sirach 13:6 (RSV)
[6] When he needs you he will deceive you, he will smile at you and give you hope. He will speak to you kindly and say, "What do you need?"

Psalm 39:13 (ESV)
[13] Look away from me, that I may smile again, before I depart and am no more!"

Job 9:27 (NIV)
27 If I say, 'I will forget my complaint, I will change my expression, and smile.'

Philippians 4:8 (RSV)
8 Finally, brethren, whatever is true, whatever is honorable, whatever is just, whatever is pure, whatever is lovely, whatever is gracious, if there is any excellence, if there is anything worthy of praise, think about these things.

Sirach 26:4 (RSV)
4 Whether rich or poor, his heart is glad, and at all times his face is cheerful.

## THE CHALLENGE

You need to be able to offer your service to others always with a smile. This will make you loved by others. They will also hold you in esteem that will lead to them respecting you and whom you represent, Our Lord Jesus Christ. A smile can bring brightness and happiness to a person's weary day. Smiles can bring sunlight into a darkness of another person's day. If one is lost and in darkness and you smile at them, you give them a sense of hope for their time of darkness. A smile from a young person invites one's peers to consider the source of that smile. If you do all things for the Lord then your smile will lead them to the Lord. Make it a choice that today you will smile at least three times to three other people. Think of the impact that will have even if they are strangers. Often people who see another person smile wonder why they are so happy and peaceful. If they stop you and ask you that question you have an opportunity to let them know that the source of your smile is the presence of the Lord in you and your values.

# 4

## CONTINUING THE JOURNEY WITH TRANSITIONAL METALS IN GROUP 5 AND 6 AND THE MEMBERS OF ACTINIDES GROUP 5f

Families are known to travel together and therefore we join up some additional members of the transitional metals in group 5 and also will be introduced to the family members of the actinides group 5f. Again with this latter group we will treat only a limited number of the elements of the family. Be ready to be enriched with additional virtues of these families.

CHEMICAL ELEMENT:             SPIRITUAL ELEMENT OF
                              VIRTUE:

Number: Name: Symbol

GROUP 5:

| 23 Vanadium | V | **V**isionary |
| 41 Niobium | Nb | **N**ot **b**oasting |
| 73 Tantalum | Ta | **Ta**bernacle Time |

ACTINIDES GROUP 5f

| 89 Actinium | Ac | **Ac**countable |
| 90 Thorium | Th | **Th**ankfulness |
| 91 Protactinium | Pa | **Pa**radise |
| 92 Uranium | U | **U**nity |

GROUP 6:

| 24 Chromium | Cr | **Cr**edibility |
| 42 Molybdenum | Mo | **Mo**rality |
| 74 Tungsten | W | **W**isdom |

GROUP 5:

#23 **V** = Vanadium **V**isionary

THE CALL

Vision takes you out of the world of small thinking. It asks you to think with the vision or viewpoint of God, which is His kingdom. It asks you to think about how you can be a creative part of building that Kingdom on earth. Vanadium is used as a metal in the making of artificial hip joints because of its ability to resist rust and breakdown. That is what happens to a person of vision. They have the ability to resist the breakdown of those who would steal their vision from them. Teens suffer more times than not, from people who want to steal their vision, their dreams, from them. When teens have the vision of the Lord no one can steal that vision from them.

## THE WORD OF GOD SAYS...

**Ezekiel 11:24 (RSV)**
[24] And the Spirit lifted me up and brought me in the vision by the Spirit of God into Chaldea, to the exiles. Then the vision that I had seen went up from me.

**Matthew 17:9 (RSV)**
[9] And as they were coming down the mountain, Jesus commanded them, "Tell no one the vision, until the Son of man is raised from the dead."

**1 Corinthians 13:12 (RSV)**
[12] For now we see in a mirror dimly, but then face to face. Now I know in part; then I shall understand fully, even as I have been fully understood.

**Ephesians 3:20 (RSV)**
[20] Now to him who by the power at work within us is able to do far more abundantly than all that we ask or think,

## THE CHALLENGE

"There is a vast difference between a person with a vision and a visionary person. The person with a vision talks little but does much. The person who is visionary talks much but does nothing." [3] This is an interesting perspective for a teen. You need to be a person with a vision so that you can do much. The much you need to do is to be a person who can lead others because of the vision you have. Vision does not just happen, it must be

---

3    Tan, P. L. (1996, c1979). *Encyclopedia of 7700 illustrations* , Garland TX: Bible Communications.

cultivated. It should be obvious that prayer is a prime requirement to develop the spiritual vision the Lord wants you to have.
He ultimately wants you to have His vision about life and not
yours. Therefore, you need to have a love for the inspiration of
the Holy Spirit, and be able to respond to the promptings of
the Spirit. In a practical sense it means that you need to be a
person with a vision of the world centered and focused on God
and His word for the direction of your life. Try to make a list
of just three things that frame your vision to follow the Lord.
Check-up on yourself in a month to see if you are living the
vision. Get it and do not let anyone take the vision from you.

#41 = **Nb** = Niobium = **N**ot **b**oasting

THE CALL

It is really hard for teens not to boast about their success, con-
quests, awards, honors and recognitions by parish, school,
community and friends. But this may not be the best way for
a young person to grow in leadership. The real teen leader at-
tracts others to follow them. Not too unlike the property that
niobium has. It is used to make magnets. It is also used to make
body jewelry used for body art because of its bluish color. This
is an activity that a teen should not boast about. It is not an
example of Christian youth leaders.

THE WORD OF GOD SAYS...

Romans 3:27 (NJB)
[27] So what becomes of our boasts? There is no room for them.
On what principle— that only actions count? No; that faith is
what counts.

1 Corinthians 5:6 (RSV)
⁶ Your boasting is not good. Do you not know that a little leaven leavens the whole lump?

1 Corinthians 9:16 (RSV)
¹⁶ For if I preach the gospel, that gives me no ground for boasting. For necessity is laid upon me. Woe to me if I do not preach the gospel!

2 Corinthians 10:15–18 (RSV)
¹⁵ We do not boast beyond limit, in other men's labors; but our hope is that as your faith increases, our field among you may be greatly enlarged, ¹⁶ so that we may preach the gospel in lands beyond you, without boasting of work already done in another's field. ¹⁷ "Let him who boasts, boast of the Lord." ¹⁸ For it is not the man who commends himself that is accepted, but the man whom the Lord commends.

James 4:16 (RSV)
¹⁶ As it is, you boast in your arrogance. All such boasting is evil.

1 John 2:16 (NIV)
¹⁶ For everything in the world—the cravings of sinful man, the lust of his eyes and the boasting of what he has and does—comes not from the Father but from the world.

THE CHALLENGE

The Lord is clear that He does not like the boastful who boast of themselves. He does not like one to act in arrogance (James 4:15-17). But He does want us to boast of Him as St. Paul tells us. That is what boasting in the Lord is all about. A teen can do this very easily. You can do it. All you have to think about is giving credit where credit is due. That is to say that, all you have to do is think of all of the incredible ways in which God has blessed you. Make a list of things that you can do, things that are your talents, things that you have learned and then when someone gives you credit thank them, and follow that with, and thanks to God for that gift. It always amazes me how so many professional male athletes when being interviewed after a successful game always seem to give God the glory. This is not boasting of oneself but boasting in the Lord. If they can do it, certainly you can too. Try it.

#73 = **Ta** = Tantalum = **Ta**bernacle Time

THE CALL:

Tantalum is an interesting element. While it may have no direct function in the human body, there are uses of this element that help the human body. Chemists tell us that tantalum is a hard, shiny, gray-blue metal that is very stable; and is not penetrated or damaged by air and water. One of the most common uses that we would know for this element is its use in surgical materials and is used in replacing bone or torn tissue; metal skull plates and fiber meshes to help mend torn nerves and muscles. Its characteristics are really important examples of the blessing of all of us taking Tabernacle time. The Lord is there in the Tabernacle and that is a stable influence in our lives. The tabernacle is a sacred place that is not penetrated by any human elements. Taking that tabernacle time is important to help you in weaknesses just like the element tantalum helps to replace injuries. Therefore, time before the tabernacle helps you repair the weakness of our lives. Count on it.

## THE WORD OF GOD SAYS...

Philippians 2:9–10 (RSV)
[9] Therefore God has highly exalted him and bestowed on him the name which is above every name, [10] that at the name of Jesus every knee should bow, in heaven and on earth and under the earth,

Hebrews 1:3 (RSV)
[3] He reflects the glory of God and bears the very stamp of his nature, upholding the universe by his word of power. When he had made purification for sins, he sat down at the right hand of the Majesty on high,

Ephesians 2:8–10 (RSV)
[8] For by grace you have been saved through faith; and this is not your own doing, it is the gift of God— [9] not because of works, lest any man should boast. [10] For we are his workmanship, created in Christ Jesus for good works, which God prepared beforehand, that we should walk in them.

2 Corinthians 6:16–17 (RSV)
[16] What agreement has the temple of God with idols? For we are the temple of the living God; as God said, "I will live in them and move among them, and I will be their God, and they shall be my people. [17] Therefore come out from them, and be separate from them, says the Lord, and touch nothing unclean; then I will welcome you,

## THE CHALLENGE

From the bible we see that God calls us to honor the presence of His son in the tabernacles of our churches. It is a great place for us to concentrate on our relationship with the Lord. This is where you can get insights into your needs for life. Take some of this "tabernacle time" and you will discover how it changes you. Think, for example, this week if you went to a church that has perpetual adoration and take some Tabernacle Time before you go on a date. Think also of coming there after you have been out on a date or other social activity. You could also do this before and or after an athletic contest. What a great way to dedicate these events in your life to the Lord. Make them important by being with Him before and after any important activities in your life. You will be different. You will be blessed. This is the week to begin this activity.

## ACTINIDES GROUP 5f

#89 **Ac** = Actinium = **Ac**countable

## THE CALL

Here is another of those radioactive elements. This one is Actinium. Checking with texts on chemistry you will discover that it is not naturally found in any living thing. You might think of it then as a "dead" element. Actually it is very active and because it is radioactive it even glows in the dark with a blue color. As with all of the radioactive elements they can cause damage to living things, usually by harming the gene pool. This is definitely an element to avoid. Because of its radioactivity and harmful effect on living things it could be said that the world of nature needs accountability from this element. For you looking at elements for your spiritual life you then need to be Accountable. This is your focus. Look first at how God's word speaks about being Accountable.

## THE WORD OF GOD SAYS...

### Romans 3:19 (RSV)

[19] Now we know that whatever the law says it speaks to those who are under the law, so that every mouth may be stopped, and the whole world may be held accountable to God.

### James 2:10 (ESV)

[10] For whoever keeps the whole law but fails in one point has become accountable for all of it.

### Ezekiel 3:18 (NIV)

[18] When I say to a wicked person, 'You will surely die,' and you do not warn them or speak out to dissuade them from their evil ways in order to save their life, that wicked person will die for their sin, and I will hold you accountable for their blood.

### Matthew 12:35–37 (RSV)

[35] The good man out of his good treasure brings forth good, and the evil man out of his evil treasure brings forth evil. [36] I tell you, on the day of judgment men will render account for every careless word they utter; [37] for by your words you will be justified, and by your words you will be condemned."

## THE CHALLENGE

Do you struggle with people you know well always asking you what you are doing or why are you doing something? That is very common for teens. They are asking you to be accountable. You may not realize that all of this began with the requirement for you as followers of the Lord to always be accountable to our Almighty God.

It is to God that we must be totally accountable. This is so in all that you say, do and are. The world wants you to ignore being accountable to God. Since He is the one and only God, who is all-powerful and all-knowing and all-present. You cannot escape it. Therefore do not even try. With God you cannot say He will never know because He will. There is no fooling God. You may fool your friends, your parents, classmates because they may not see you all the time as God does.

There is an old expression that you "can fool some of the people some of the time, but not all of the people all of the time." If you are not accountable you are probably on the road of being a phony. People will soon find out and then you will really suffer. You end up fooling only yourself.

Since you have been accountable since you were a small child you are not a stranger to being accountable. You can handle what the world wants and therefore, you can and should handle being spiritually accountable to the Lord. The great reason is that it will make you a holy person. What a blessing that is!

It is when you are accountable to the Lord that you really grow in goodness. Then you can be a powerful example to those around you. One day this week sit down and write a list of four people that you will be accountable to for your behavior. Make the Lord the first one on the list and tell Him you will be accountable for your good behavior for the next day. At the end of the day check in with God and tell him how you were accountable. It will teach you how to live out your responsibilities.

#90 **Th** = Thorium = **Th**ankfulness

## THE CALL

Thorium in nature is an element, that while radioactive, does have a useful purpose. That purpose is in generating energy. Scientists say that thorium has more untapped energy than all of the uranium and other fossil fuels. This is an interesting aspect of an element, having a hidden value not expected. In God's world you have a hidden value in the virtue of Thankfulness. It too is a hidden source of great spiritual energy for those who are thankful. God's word gives us some interesting insights in being thankful.

## THE WORD OF GOD SAYS...

Philippians 1:3–6 (RSV)
[3] I thank my God in all my remembrance of you, [4] always in every prayer of mine for you all making my prayer with joy, [5] thankful for your partnership in the gospel from the first day until now. [6] And I am sure that he who began a good work in you will bring it to completion at the day of Jesus Christ.

Colossians 3:15-16 (RSV)
[15] And let the peace of Christ rule in your hearts, to which indeed you were called in the one body. And be thankful. [16] Let the word of Christ dwell in you richly, teach and admonish one another in all wisdom, and sing psalms and hymns and spiritual songs with thankfulness in your hearts to God.

Colossians 4:2 (RSV)
[2] Continue steadfastly in prayer, being watchful in it with thanksgiving.

Hebrews 12:28-29 (NIV)

[28] Therefore, since we are receiving a kingdom that cannot be shaken, let us be thankful, and so worship God acceptably with reverence and awe, [29] for our "God is a consuming fire."

## THE CHALLENGE

It is clear to see that God's word gives you many reasons to be thankful. This is true even if you are having difficult times in your life. Maybe it has been a bad day at school because of a difficult exam. It may have been a classmate who was mean to you in some way. In all things it is a blessing to trust God at all times. Being thankful in these times is far better than being a complainer or whiner.

Being thankful breed's things you are thankful for. It is very much like success. Success breeds success. You cannot be a whiner and a thankful person at the same time.

Being thankful is something you acquire by doing. You are not born a thankful person. That means that you have to be taught to be thankful. What do you do to get started in the art of being thankful? First know that it is a habit you can develop in your life. Next and most important, thank God for everything starting with thanking Him for the gift of life.

It is absolutely amazing that when you are thankful you also become a joyful person. Try it some time and see what happens when you thank someone for just being your friend. Thank God today for that gift of life and then also thank a friend who has been faithful to you. Just say to someone that you are thankful for them. Watch the reaction you get. It is when you are thankful especially to God that you even see things the way God sees all things. As His holy word told you, be thankful in all things.

Don Moen sings a beautiful hymn about thanks. It is called "Give Thanks With a Grateful Heart". Meditate on the lyrics. Here they are:

Give Thanks (Songwriters: Smith, Henry)

Give thanks with a grateful heart
Give thanks to the Holy One
Give thanks because He's given Jesus Christ, His Son

Give thanks with a grateful heart
Give thanks to the Holy One
Give thanks because He's given Jesus Christ, His Son

And now let the weak say, "I am strong"
Let the poor say, "I am rich
Because of what the Lord has done for us"

And now let the weak say, "I am strong"
Let the poor say, "I am rich
Because of what the Lord has done for us"

Give thanks with a grateful heart
Give thanks to the Holy One
Give thanks because He's given Jesus Christ, His Son

Give thanks with a grateful heart
Give thanks to the Holy One
Give thanks because He's given Jesus Christ, His Son

And now let the weak say, "I am strong"
Let the poor say, "I am rich
Because of what the Lord has done for us"

And now let the weak say, "I am strong"
Let the poor say, "I am rich
Because of what the Lord has done for us"
Give thanks

We give thanks to You oh Lord
We give thanks

#91 **Pa** = Protactinium = **Pa**radise

## THE CALL

This is a most interesting element. It is very rare, also toxic, and radioactive. Unless you are in a laboratory doing scientific research you will not run into it. Its name is also very interesting. Pro comes from the Greek word for first "protos", and then actinium. Therefore, put the two pieces together and the name means "parent of actinium." Since it is so rare there are no biological uses for this element. But it does give us an interesting metaphor spiritually, the symbol for Protactinium is Pa, which for us means Paradise. Not bad when you think about it, because Paradise is not rare for us, but our destination given us by God. God is, for us our Father, and therefore, is the source of our spiritual home, paradise.

## THE WORD OF GOD

Luke 23:39–44 (RSV)

[39] One of the criminals who were hanged railed at him, saying, "Are you not the Christ? Save yourself and us!" [40] But the other rebuked him, saying, "Do you not fear God, since you are under the same sentence of condemnation? [41] And we indeed justly; for we are receiving the due reward of our deeds; but this man has done nothing wrong." [42] And he said, "Jesus, remember me when you come into your kingdom." [43] And he said to him, "Truly, I say to you, today you will be with me in Paradise." [44] It was now about the sixth hour, and there was darkness over the whole land until the ninth hour.

2 Corinthians 12:3 (RSV)

[3] And I know that this man was caught up into Paradise—whether in the body or out of the body I do not know, God knows—

Revelation 2:7 (RSV)

[7] He who has an ear, let him hear what the Spirit says to the churches. To him who conquers I will grant to eat of the tree of life, which is in the paradise of God.'

Sirach 40:27 (NAB)

[27] The fear of God is a paradise of blessings; its canopy, all that is glorious.

## THE CHALLENGE

Paradise, as mentioned, is not rare, but a blessing and God's word affirms that for you. It is a place to which He invites you to spend your eternity there. You have seen in His holy words of scripture that it is a reward for a good life.

This reward has several things to hope for and therefore, something to strive to attain by a good life. From studying God's word you can gather a few of the blessings of heaven. We know that it will be filled with the presence of God, known as the beatific vision, that is gift enough. But there are other blessings of heaven.

Since it is the dwelling of God it has to be a place of great and unimaginable beauty. It will be a place where you will be able to share God's presence with those you loved on earth. Did you lose a classmate or friend in high school? Were you close to them? They will be there to enjoy. It will be a place of absolute peace and harmony. Just think you will not be suffering from any conflicts or pain there. It would not be heaven if there were.

One final blessing of heaven is that it will be a place where you will encounter the Lord and be able to offer Him praise and thanks. Remember the scripture that tells of the angels singing, "holy, holy, holy is the Lord."

This is your call. Therefore, now is the time to work hard to attain it. Remember it is a reward for a good life. Make a point today to do some good work for another person on earth and to pray for a soul in purgatory to be released into heaven so that person can also enjoy the presence of God. Do it and be blessed.

#92 **U** = Uranium = **U**nity

THE CALL

You know this element well. Uranium is talked about all the time. In your classes you have heard of the use of uranium in nuclear power plants all over the world. There are generally three forms of uranium, one of which is known as Uranium 235, and this is the one that can be used to generate nuclear power. It, like most of the more recently named elements, is radioactive. Since it is radioactive, as you might expect, studies have been made to see what effect it might have on your health. Interestingly scientists have found that the natural levels of uranium have no harmful radiation effects for humans. It is only a problem when someone takes in unusually large amounts of uranium. The name came from the planet Uranus. Since uranium is used as a source of energy generation in nature it is only logical that we could say that spiritually our symbol for Uranium, U, for us means Unity, which is a source of energy for the Body of Christ. Let us take a look at what God has to say in the scriptures about unity.

THE WORD OF GOD SAYS...

Psalm 133:1 (RSV)
[1] Behold, how good and pleasant it is when brothers dwell in unity!

Ephesians 4:1–3 (RSV)
[1] I therefore, a prisoner for the Lord, beg you to lead a life worthy of the calling to which you have been called, [2] with all lowliness and meekness, with patience, forbearing one another in love, [3] eager to maintain the unity of the Spirit in the bond of peace.

Ephesians 4:13 (RSV)
[13] until we all attain to the unity of the faith and of the knowledge of the Son of God, to mature manhood, to the measure of the stature of the fullness of Christ.

1 Peter 3:8 (RSV)
[8] Finally, all of you, have unity of spirit, sympathy, love of the brethren, a tender heart and a humble mind.

John 17:20-23 (NIV)
[20] "My prayer is not for them alone. I pray also for those who will believe in me through their message [21] that all of them may be one, Father, just as you are in me and I am in you. May they also be in us so that the world may believe that you have sent me. [22] I have given them the glory that you gave me, that they may be one as we are one—[23] I in them and you in me—so that they may be brought to complete unity. Then the world will know that you sent me and have loved them even as you have loved me.

Ephesians 4:3-6 (NIV)
[3] Make every effort to keep the unity of the Spirit through the bond of peace. [4] There is one body and one Spirit, just as you were called to one hope when you were called; [5] one Lord, one

faith, one baptism; [6] one God and Father of all, who is over all and through all and in all.

## THE CHALLENGE

Jesus, in our scriptures above, is telling us all about unity. It is as if He is asking you to be a full, powerful, effective member of "Team Jesus". To be a member of that team you have to be in unity with Him and His teachings. If you do you will be members of a very powerful team. This team is needed today to fight all of the attacks against our Church. There are always those who do not want you to succeed as a member of "Team Jesus". Do not let it happen, be strong and united to your brothers and sisters in the faith and to the teachings of the Church. This is a power no force can come against.

Recall the requirements for this unity as given in St. Paul's letter to the Ephesians. We are called to unity of one body; one spirit; one hope; one Lord; one faith; one baptism; one God and Father of all. You are given these seven steps to unity. They are given to you and strengthen you by the Church that Jesus established.

Your task and call then, is to put these into practical use. Try for the next week to pray for unity in one of these steps each day this week. Then after you pray for each step try to see how you can do that step on the day you pray for it.

GROUP 6:

#24: **Cr** = Chromium = **Cr**edibility

THE CALL

To be a person of credibility is to say, in the world of the Lord, that they are faithful and trustworthy to the Christian Creed. The Catholic teen needs to be faithful to the Creed we proclaim each Sunday at Mass, which comes to us from the Council of Nicea (325 AD). The Credible teen who stands for the Creed is a strong person indeed. Very much like the uses of chromium. Chromium, used in plating, produces a hard, beautiful surface and prevents corrosion. You may be familiar with it in parts of your car that you have chromed, for example, hub caps; and bumpers; engine parts. You do that so that they will have that shiny surface and be corrosion free. That is what a CREED does for a Church, gives it beauty and keeps the Church from corrosion.

THE WORD OF GOD SAYS...

4 Maccabees 7:9 (RSV)
9 You, father, strengthened our loyalty to the law through your glorious endurance, and you did not abandon the holiness which you praised, but by your deeds you made your words of divine philosophy credible.

1 Chronicles 29:17 (RSV)
17 I know, my God, that thou triest the heart, and hast pleasure in uprightness; in the uprightness of my heart I have freely offered all these things, and now I have seen thy people, who are present here, offering freely and joyously to thee.

1 Corinthians 7:25 (RSV)
[25] Now concerning the unmarried, I have no command of the Lord, but I give my opinion as one who by the Lord's mercy is trustworthy.

Sirach 46:15 (RSV)
[15] By his faithfulness he was proved to be a prophet, and by his words he became known as a trustworthy seer.

2 Timothy 2:11-13 (ESV)
[11] The saying is trustworthy, for: If we have died with him, we will also live with him; [12] if we endure, we will also reign with him; if we deny him, he also will deny us; [13] if we are faithless, he remains faithful—

Exodus 18:21 (RSV)
[21] Moreover choose able men from all the people, such as fear God, men who are trustworthy and who hate a bribe; and place such men over the people as rulers of thousands, of hundreds, of fifties, and of tens.

Psalm 111:7 (RSV)
[7] The works of his hands are faithful and just; all his precepts are trustworthy.

THE CHALLENGE

Teens of the millennial generation have a hard time with credibility which means being trustworthy. Could it be that the above is true because teens do not know how to hold fast to the Christian Creed. We all need to take in hand the Creed of our Church so that we can have a solid basis for our actions in life. The Creed removes any doubts about what we believe. It is also a basis for freedom in our lives since it removes any need to have multiple options of what to believe about God. We need the creed to give us that basis, just as chromium is needed to give emeralds their green color and rubies their red color. Without the chromium you would not be able to identify the emerald or the ruby. So with the creed, without it, you cannot identify the follower of Christ. Take some time this week to read the Creed that you recite each Sunday at Mass. Read it slowly and see how it gives your faith this solid basis.

#42: **Mo** = Molybdenum = **Mo**rality

THE CALL

Morality or good conduct, is necessary for strength in the life that God calls you to live. Molybdenum is necessary to give incredible strength to the hardness of steel. You have heard of the "man of steel" most probably. The Superman image is well known as a man of great strength. Both the element and the capacity it has for giving strength is the lesson nature gives you to seek that which will give you the strength in life. It is your morality, your good conduct, that you live by in all of your decisions that makes you a person of steel for the Lord.

THE WORD OF GOD SAYS...

1 Timothy 4:12 (RSV)
[12] Let no one despise your youth, but set the believers an example in speech and conduct, in love, in faith, in purity.

1 Peter 1:15 (RSV)
[15] but as he who called you is holy, be holy yourselves in all your conduct;

Romans 13:13 (RSV)
[13] let us conduct ourselves becomingly as in the day, not in reveling and drunkenness, not in debauchery and licentiousness, not in quarreling and jealousy.

Sirach 11:26 (RSV)
[26] For it is easy in the sight of the Lord to reward a man on the day of death according to his conduct.

Romans 13:3 (RSV)
[3] For rulers are not a terror to good conduct, but to bad. Would you have no fear of him who is in authority? Then do what is good, and you will receive his approval,

Colossians 4:5 (RSV)
[5] Conduct yourselves wisely toward outsiders, making the most of the time.

## THE CHALLENGE

It is not easy to talk about morality or good conduct, because morality is not easy. But it is what gives strength to your character. Having good morality means that you stand for your beliefs and your conduct and choices in life are in agreement with God's commandments. This makes it easy to live a moral life. Just be faithful to the commandments. Doing that gives you a freedom in making decisions. So living a good moral life is pleasing to God. It is also a peaceful living that you receive for living that moral life. You see when your morality is lived, it is really a form of guidance for life, and because your morality is in agreement with what the Lord expects, then this gives you protection in life. Take time one day this week to look over your choices. Ask just one question: were they in agreement with God's expectations of a son or daughter of the Lord? If not, make a decision right then to make an important change in your life regarding that bad moral decision. This will save you from sin and protect you from exposure to additional harm. It is a life of good conduct that the Lord blesses. Live it now.

#74: **W** = Tungsten = **W**isdom

THE CALL

Probably the only time you actually come in contact with Tungsten is if you have had some dental work done. If you have had some of your teeth drilled to put in fillings the drill probably has tungsten in it. You might be interested to know that the symbol for tungsten is W, since the Latin name for this element is Wolfram. It is also said that this element is used by a small number of enzymes. But this is not too clearly seen in humans. It is a strong metal and has the highest melting point of any element. This is why the symbol helps us to relate it to Wisdom. When you have wisdom, you have a "high spiritual melting point." This could easily mean for you that, when you have this gift of the Holy Spirit, you have an incredible strength of the Lord. This gift of Wisdom helps you to know the purpose and plan of God.

## THE WORD OF GOD SAYS...

Psalm 37:30 (RSV)
[30] The mouth of the righteous utters wisdom, and his tongue speaks justice.

Proverbs 1:7 (RSV)
[7] The fear of the LORD is the beginning of knowledge; fools despise wisdom and instruction.

Proverbs 2:6 (RSV)
[6] For the LORD gives wisdom; from his mouth come knowledge and understanding.

Proverbs 2:1–2 (RSV)
[1] My son, if you receive my words and treasure up my commandments with you, [2] making your ear attentive to wisdom and inclining your heart to understanding.

Psalm 111:10 (RSV)
[10] The fear of the LORD is the beginning of wisdom; a good understanding have all those who practice it. His praise endures forever!

1 Corinthians 2:13 (RSV)
[13] And we impart this in words not taught by human wisdom but taught by the Spirit, interpreting spiritual truths to those who possess the Spirit.

Sirach 1:1–4 (RSV)
[1] All wisdom comes from the Lord and is with him forever. [2] The sand of the sea, the drops of rain, and the days of

eternity—who can count them? [3] The height of heaven, the breadth of the earth, the abyss, and wisdom—who can search them out? [4] Wisdom was created before all things, and prudent understanding from eternity.

James 1:5 (RSV)

[5] If any of you lacks wisdom, let him ask God, who gives to all men generously and without reproaching, and it will be given him.

## THE CHALLENGE

You know how hard it is to be a teen in the world today. There are so many conflicting opinions that are putting pressure on you. Most of them are really false and lack the wisdom of God. You can avoid all of the confusion if you will let the Lord guide you. This primary guidance comes from the teachings of the Church. You do not want to be controlled by the false theories and ideas of the world, which is in confusion. If you agree with God then you will be on the road to knowing the ways He wants you to live. Then you will have His Wisdom given to you.

You can do this if you will let God's Wisdom be reflected in your goodness each day. Therefore, the next time you are confronted with an opinion that is not of God, ask the Holy Spirit for an increase in this great spiritual gift. Learn what God wants by studying His Word in the Bible. Remember as the book of Sirach tells us, that "all wisdom comes from God." You can be a person of Wisdom if you walk each day in the way the Lord instructs you through the Church.

# 5

## TRANSITIONAL METALS FAMILY CONTINUES WITH GROUPS 7, 8 AND 9 AND THE RELATED VIRTUES

The Transitional Metals are really a large family and more to come. We experience in this chapter the members of groups 7, 8 and 9. They are paired with the virtues that relate the symbols of these groups.

CHEMICAL ELEMENT:          SPIRITUAL ELEMENT OF VIRTUE:

Number: Name: Symbol

GROUP 7:
25 Manganese      Mn      **M**oral **n**orms
43 Technetium      Tc      **T**rue **c**ontrition
75 Rhenium      Re      **Re**verence

GROUP 8:

| 26 Iron | Fe | **Fe**llowship |
|---------|-----|-----------------|
| 44 Ruthenium | Ru | **Ru**thlike |
| 76 Osmium | Os | **Os**tracize |

GROUP 9:

| 27 Cobalt | Co | **Co**mpassion |
|-----------|-----|-----------------|
| 45 Rhodium | Rh | **R**adical **h**umility |
| 77 Iridium | Ir | **Ir**reproachable |

GROUP 7:

#25 **Mn** = Manganese = **M**oral **n**orms

THE CALL

All are called to live a faith-filled life and make choices based on solid MORAL NORMS given us by the Church so that we can have clarity about choices in life. Moral norms set the boundaries of what we do and what we decide. Manganese is essential for many enzymes (proteins that are produced by living cells and catalyze specific biochemical reactions at body temperatures) to work in your body, such as vitamin B 1. Without the enzyme the body function cannot take place. Without the Moral Norms of your faith, you cannot function faithfully as God has asked you. Moral Norms help one to live in godliness. Godliness leads to holiness of life.

THE WORD OF GOD SAYS...

1 Corinthians 15:33 (RSV)
[33] Do not be deceived: "Bad company ruins good morals."

1 Timothy 4:7 (RSV)
[7] Have nothing to do with godless and silly myths. Train yourself in godliness.

1 Timothy 6:11 (RSV)
[11] But as for you, man of God, shun all this; aim at righteousness, godliness, faith, love, steadfastness, gentleness.

2 Peter 1:3 (RSV)
[3] His divine power has granted to us all things that pertain to life and godliness, through the knowledge of him who called us to his own glory and excellence,

Titus 1:1 (RSV)
[1] Paul, a servant of God and an apostle of Jesus Christ, to further the faith of God's elect and their knowledge of the truth which accords with godliness,

Exodus 19:8 (RSV)
[8] And all the people answered together and said, "All that the LORD has spoken we will do." And Moses reported the words of the people to the LORD.

Matthew 5:17 (RSV)
[17] "Think not that I have come to abolish the law and the prophets; I have come not to abolish them but to fulfill them.

Matthew 5:20 (RSV)
[20] For I tell you, unless your righteousness exceeds that of the scribes and Pharisees, you will never enter the kingdom of heaven.

John 14:15 (RSV)
15 "If you love me, you will keep my commandments.

## THE CHALLENGE

Teens are often caught in situations that would cause them to
do something not in accord with God's commandments. That
is why moral norms are so important. They set the boundaries
of choices for you and that is a neat way for you to handle difficult moral situations. You do not have to compromise your beliefs. You need only to live them. Go ahead and blame God for
your saying no to sex, drugs, and pornography. He can handle
the blame, and you can then handle the freedom of conscience
that you have not sinned, but followed God faithfully. Make a
list of the times that someone tried to tempt you to do something against God's law. Keep it and note each time that you
are successful in not falling to that temptation. Celebrate how
it feels to make the right choice based on the Moral Norms of
your faith taught to you by the Church.

#43: **Tc** = Technetium = **T**rue **c**ontrition

## THE CALL

Technetium is rarely found on earth. It has no biological role
in our bodies but it does have uses in analysis in our bodies,
much like x-rays which are used to discover internal problems.
Therefore, the use of an isotope of this element can be used
for diagnosis within your bodies. Interesting that it is used
in analysis. That is what true contrition does for your souls.
When you have true contrition, you are on a path of constantly
analyzing your life in relationship to the expectations the Lord

has for you. Remember the Lord is always looking for your spiritual health. He will always accept your true contrition, and not just a convenient contrition.

## THE WORD OF GOD SAYS...

Psalm 51:17 (RSV)
[17] The sacrifice acceptable to God is a broken spirit; a broken and contrite heart, O God, thou wilt not despise.

Isaiah 57:15 (RSV)
[15] For thus says the high and lofty One who inhabits eternity, whose name is Holy: "I dwell in the high and holy place, and also with him who is of a contrite and humble spirit, to revive the spirit of the humble, and to revive the heart of the contrite.

Isaiah 66:2 (RSV)
[2] All these things my hand has made, and so all these things are mine, says the LORD. But this is the man to whom I will look, he that is humble and contrite in spirit, and trembles at my word.

Psalm 34:18 (RSV)
[18] The LORD is near to the brokenhearted, and saves the crushed in spirit.

Psalm 50:8 (D-R)
[8] For behold thou hast loved truth: the uncertain and hidden things of thy wisdom thou hast made manifest to me.

REV. FRED R. GAGLIA, Ph.D.

## THE CHALLENGE

Thomas a Kempis tell us that "Happy is the man who can throw off the weight of every care and recollect himself in holy contrition. Happy is the man who casts from him all that can stain or burden his conscience."[4]

When you have that true contrition you are getting to the zones of life that are not in unison with God's expectations for you. It is a first step in the process of receiving forgiveness from God. As you know, in the sacrament of Reconciliation, you need to have this true contrition to receive the effect of the forgiveness that the Lord so desires to give you. Now is a good time to consider if you have true contrition or you are just afraid of the punishment for sin in your life. True and perfect contrition means you are sorry for what you have done because you love God. Seek that true contrition so that you may always be worthy before the Lord. It is not easy to say "I am contrite" because it requires an admission that I did something not in line with God's law. But the blessing of it is the forgiveness that comes from the Lord. It is a freedom from guilt and a sense of being spiritually clean before God. Have you had times when, because of one of your actions, and you did not feel so good? Then that is the time to seek true contrition. Just admit the fault and seek the Lord's forgiveness. He never turns down a person with true contrition. This week would be a good time to examine, or look at your life, and see if there is an area you need cleansed. Pray for that true contrition. Seek God's forgiveness. Experience His gift of being freed. You will be happy you did.

4    Thomas à Kempis. (1996). *The imitation of Christ* (40). Oak Harbor, WA: Logos Research Systems.

#75: **Re** = Rhenium = **Re**verence

## THE CALL

Rhenium is one of the rarest elements in earth's crust. It was named after the Rhine river and has the symbol Re. When added to high-temperature super alloys it is used to make jet engine parts. It is also said that the isotopes (radioactive forms of the element) are used for treatment of liver cancer. Just think for a moment when you have any spiritual cancer, e.g., addictions, you probably need some treatment for that "cancer". Think of that treatment with the symbol of Rhenium, namely Re =the treatment is reverence for the Lord.

## THE WORD OF GOD SAYS...

1 Peter 3:13–15 (RSV)
[13] Now who is there to harm you if you are zealous for what is right? [14] But even if you do suffer for righteousness' sake, you will be blessed. Have no fear of them, nor be troubled, [15] but in your hearts reverence Christ as Lord. Always be prepared to make a defense to any one who calls you to account for the hope that is in you, yet do it with gentleness and reverence;

Hebrews 12:28 (RSV)
[28] Therefore let us be grateful for receiving a kingdom that cannot be shaken, and thus let us offer to God acceptable worship, with reverence and awe.

Ephesians 5:21 (RSV)
[21] Be subject to one another out of reverence for Christ.

1 Peter 1:17–19 (NAB)

[17] Now if you invoke as Father him who judges impartially according to each one's works, conduct yourselves with reverence during the time of your sojourning, [18] realizing that you were ransomed from your futile conduct, handed on by your ancestors, not with perishable things like silver or gold [19] but with the precious blood of Christ as of a spotless unblemished lamb.

Psalm 2:11–12 (NASB)

[11] Worship the LORD with reverence And rejoice with trembling. [12] Do homage to the Son, that He not become angry, and you perish *in* the way, For His wrath may soon be kindled. How blessed are all who take refuge in Him!

THE APPLICATION

We need to think always of having reverence for the Lord. This is expressed in practical ways by our reverence during the celebration of the Mass; our reverence for the name of the Lord and not use it in any sinful way; reverence for your parents. Remember to honor your father and mother, the fourth commandment, is the only commandment that comes with a promise. Read it in the bible and you will be blessed because of your reverence for your parents. Also reverence and honor your bodies and not let them be used in any way for sinful purposes. For example reverence the gift of your eyes and do not offend against reverence for your eyes by having them being infected with a cancer of pornography. God blesses you when you do have reverence in all situations of your life. You will be blessed if you reverence the Lord and it will teach you the blessing of reverencing others as well. This week, on Wednesday, make it a point to show reverence for the Lord by doing an act of penance for ever having offended Him by a misuse of your eyes. You might therefore, on this day fast from viewing the internet. Do that as your act of reverence to the Lord. Remember doing difficult things are an act of sacrifice. Acts of sacrifice for the Lord always receive a blessing from Him.

GROUP 8

#26: **Fe** = Iron = **Fe**llowship

THE CALL

What a great gift we have in the Church when we belong to its fellowship. Fellowship with God is a necessary first so that you can keep your faith life fresh and exciting. Fe (ferrous in Latin for iron) is important in all of life. For example in humans iron is an important part of the molecule hemoglobin in our blood to help it carry life-giving oxygen. In nature iron is a necessary component in steel. And we know what strength steel has. So it is with fellowship, it gives strength to your relationships. You should not live your life as a teen without solid good Christian fellowship. Let your fellowship with the Lord be the beginning. Follow that with strong fellowship within a loving Christian community.

THE WORD OF GOD SAYS...

2 Corinthians 13:13–14
[13] All the saints greet you. [14] The grace of the Lord Jesus Christ and the love of God and the fellowship of the Holy Spirit be with you all.

1 Corinthians 1:9 (RSV)
[9] God is faithful, by whom you were called into the fellowship of his Son, Jesus Christ our Lord.

1 John 1:5–7 (RSV)
[5] This is the message we have heard from him and proclaim to you, that God is light and in him is no darkness at all. [6] If we say we have fellowship with him while we walk in darkness, we lie and do not live according to the truth; [7] but if we walk in the light, as he is in the light, we have fellowship with one another, and the blood of Jesus his Son cleanses us from all sin.

Acts 2:41–42 (RSV)
[41] So those who received his word were baptized, and there were added that day about three thousand souls. [42] And they devoted themselves to the apostles' teaching and fellowship, to the breaking of bread and the prayers.

THE CHALLENGE

A great need exists for teens to be in Christian fellowship. Just look at what God says in the scriptures about it. Look at the blessings that He promises to you. I Cor. 1:9 "God is faithful; by him you were called into the fellowship of his Son, Jesus Christ our Lord." God is faithful and we get our fellowship with Christ through the great power of the Holy Spirit. Then consider that if you are not in fellowship you are really walking in darkness and alone. Not a way to go in this world of sin and evilness. Be a bright light, a light strong as steel, to help lead yourself to Christ and to help lead others to Christ. This can be done easily in fellowship. Seek to see if there is a youth fellowship at your parish church. If yours does not have a fellowship group, seek it in another parish. This is where you need to be. It is the place to be to help you deepen your prayer life and your knowledge and love of God. It is the place where you will experience the Holy Spirit to help you discern what it is God wants for you in the future. What a great place for a teen to be helped to make good moral decisions. Go for it!

#44: **Ru** = Ruthenium = **Ru**th-like

THE CALL

Ruthenium is a silvery white metal that does not tarnish. What an attribute to have. In the world of the spiritual "Ru" can stand for "Ruth-like", in the model of Ruth of the scriptures. Ruth did not tarnish either. She is known in the bible as the widow who spoke to Naomi her mother-in-law, who was also widowed, and had lost not only her husband, but also her sons. The scriptures tell us of her friendship and loyalty. It is perhaps the best case to describe virtuous friendship and loyalty in all of spiritual writings.

THE WORD OF GOD SAYS...

Ruth 1:16–17 (RSV)
[16] But Ruth said, "Entreat me not to leave you or to return from following you; for where you go I will go, and where you lodge I will lodge; your people shall be my people, and your God my God; [17] where you die I will die, and there will I be buried. May the LORD do so to me and more also if even death parts me from you."

Psalm 25:14 (RSV)
[14] The friendship of the LORD is for those who fear him, and he makes known to them his covenant.

Proverbs 22:24 (RSV)

[24] Make no friendship with a man given to anger, nor go with a wrathful man,

James 4:4 (RSV)

[4] Unfaithful creatures! Do you not know that friendship with the world is enmity with God? Therefore whoever wishes to be a friend of the world makes himself an enemy of God.

Sirach 22:20–22 (RSV)

[20] One who throws a stone at birds scares them away, and one who reviles a friend will break off the friendship. [21] Even if you have drawn your sword against a friend, do not despair, for a renewal of friendship is possible. [22] If you have opened your mouth against your friend, do not worry, for reconciliation is possible; but as for reviling, arrogance, disclosure of secrets, or a treacherous blow— in these cases any friend will flee.

Psalm 109:4 (RSV)

[4] In return for my love they accuse me, even as I make prayer for them.

## THE CHALLENGE

A teen's responsibilities are many and sometimes overwhelming. One of them is to be a true friend and loyal to that friend. "Faith is no subjective fancy, but demands loyalty to what Christ taught his followers." (The Catholic Catechism) You need to learn to have a true friend as Ruth was to Naomi. If you can be true to a friend in school or in sports and also be loyal to that person, then you have passed the training ground to be loyal to Christ. If you do not have any experience of keeping friends then you will not be able to be a friend of Christ. If you are not loyal to a friend in life it will be difficult to be loyal to Christ. You need that friendship and loyalty to Christ so that you might learn and be prepared to receive the greatest gifts that God wants to give you. It is the way you can be successful in friendships with your peers. When you are, the word gets around that you are a loyal person. What a way to be known by your peers and your parents. Take some time to say a prayer of gratitude to God for at least three of your true friends.

#76: **Os** = Osmium = **Os**tracize

THE CALL

Osmium has a nice sounding name, but it is a highly poisonous substance and can cause some serious health problems such as lung congestion, skin damage, and eye problems such as causes the eyes to really tear up. The symbol for Osmium is Os and this reminds you of a problem that you need to turn around to be virtuous. The virtue is not to ostracize people.

THE WORD:

Matthew 7:22 (RSV)
²² On that day many will say to me, 'Lord, Lord, did we not prophesy in your name, and cast out demons in your name, and do many mighty works in your name?'

Matthew 9:33 (RSV)
³³ And when the demon had been cast out, the dumb man spoke; and the crowds marveled, saying, "Never was anything like this seen in Israel."

Mark 16:17 (RSV)

[17] And these signs will accompany those who believe: in my name they will cast out demons; they will speak in new tongues.

Luke 6:22 (RSV)

[22] "Blessed are you when men hate you, and when they exclude you and revile you, and cast out your name as evil, on account of the Son of man!

Luke 13:32 (RSV)

[32] And he said to them, "Go and tell that fox, 'Behold, I cast out demons and perform cures today and tomorrow, and the third day I finish my course.

John 6:37 (RSV)

[37] All that the Father gives me will come to me; and him who comes to me I will not cast out.

Luke 5:12–16 (RSV)

[12] While he was in one of the cities, there came a man full of leprosy; and when he saw Jesus, he fell on his face and besought him, "Lord, if you will, you can make me clean." [13] And he stretched out his hand, and touched him, saying, "I will; be clean." And immediately the leprosy left him. [14] And he charged him to tell no one; but "go and show yourself to the priest, and make an offering for your cleansing, as Moses commanded, for a proof to the people." [15] But so much the more the report went abroad concerning him; and great multitudes gathered to hear and to be healed of their infirmities. [16] But he withdrew to the wilderness and prayed.

## THE CHALLENGE

All too often today we have a tendency to do as the people at the time of Jesus and we OSTRACIZE or cast out people who really need us. Have you ever put aside someone at school? Perhaps you neglect a student who is new and needs someone to be a friend. They know no one and you can make them feel welcome. This is what Jesus did with the lepers in the scripture. He was not afraid to be contaminated when He touched them. You will note that His touch, His presence, was a healing for those lepers. Notice that the Bible also says that we should cast out certain people who do not follow the way of the Lord. Jesus is very strong that you be faithful to Him in all that He teaches. Jesus is always casting out devils from people's lives. Therefore, there are two ways to be aware of how God wants to work through you. "Cast out" or avoid those who do things of evil. Also you can do something practical by your presence and welcome a new student or one struggling with classes. This will be a healing for a fellow classmate. This week make a special effort to seek out a student who needs your help. It does not matter if it is class study material or maybe it is help with a skill you have on an athletic team. Think of the healing and welcome you could be to that person.

## GROUP 9

#27: **Co** = Cobalt = **Co**mpassion

## THE CALL

Ever have your mother tell you to take your vitamins? Well, if she asked you to take Vitamin B-12, guess what? It contains cobalt. Vitamins are important for our lives to have some kind of extra vitality. If you are spiritually a vital person then you will be a person with compassion. This is often an under recognized virtue in teens. I have always loved when a difficult situation arises and watch teens respond. There was a situation when I was pastor that a youth minister's son had been injured in an accident and needed incredible assistance, not only medical but also financial. I mentioned it to the teens and asked them to seek ways for our parish to help. The compassion that was displayed was astounding. The young person did not even live near the parish that they were asked to help and they did. That is compassion.

THE WORD OF GOD SAYS...

2 Corinthians 1:3 (NAB)
[3] Blessed be the God and Father of our Lord Jesus Christ, the Father of compassion and God of all encouragement,

I John 3: 17 (NAB)
[17] If someone who has worldly means sees a brother in need and refuses him compassion, how can the love of God remain in him?

Luke 6:36 (NJB)
[36] 'Be compassionate just as your Father is compassionate.

Psalm 145:9 (RSV)
[9] The LORD is good to all, and his compassion is over all that he has made.

Colossians 3:12 (RSV)
[12] Put on then, as God's chosen ones, holy and beloved, compassion, kindness, lowliness, meekness, and patience.

Matthew 15:32 (RSV)
[32] Then Jesus called his disciples to him and said, "I have compassion on the crowd, because they have been with me now three days, and have nothing to eat; and I am unwilling to send them away hungry, lest they faint on the way."

## THE CHALLENGE

If the Lord is good to everyone, and we are called to follow the Lord, then we need, as He tells us, to be compassionate to others. Notice when we give compassion then we are promised that the love of God remains in us. What a blessing indeed. Notice that God's word says that if you are compassionate you will also receive from God the gift of encouragement. Seems when you do, as the Lord has done, you end up being the one who is also blessed. Perhaps today is the day to look to see how you can have compassion for someone else. I know that older people who are in rest homes are generally very lonely people. They begin to sparkle when a young person comes to just say hello. What a simple way to express the compassion you have. Watch the joy you see on the face of that older person. You may be the only person other than staff who comes to visit them. When you have made the visit and leave just remember the feeling inside of you. This is an expression of the blessing that God gives to those who give compassion.

#45: **Rh** = Rhodium = **R**adical **h**umility

THE CALL

Radical humility is the recognition that you are a person who really knows oneself. You know what are the gifts that God has given you. You know how to use them to help build up others. You do not pretend to be something that you are not. That is radical humility. Rhodium is a metal element that is hard and durable, in the chemical world, that would mean that is has radical humility. It is what it is and not something else. Humility must be radical so that it does not admit of space for the evil one to disguise the real virtue.

THE WORD

Proverbs 15:33 (RSV)
[33] The fear of the LORD is instruction in wisdom, and humility goes before honor.

1 Peter 5:5 (RSV)
[5] Likewise you that are younger be subject to the elders. Clothe yourselves, all of you, with humility toward one another, for "God opposes the proud, but gives grace to the humble."

James 3:13 (NIV)
[13] Who is wise and understanding among you? Let them show it by their good life, by deeds done in the humility that comes from wisdom.

Sirach 10:28 (RSV)
[28] My son, glorify yourself with humility, and ascribe to yourself honor according to your worth.

Sirach 3:17–19 (RSV)

[17] My son, perform your tasks in meekness; then you will be loved by those whom God accepts. [18] The greater you are, the more you must humble yourself; so you will find favor in the sight of the Lord. [19] For great is the might of the Lord; he is glorified by the humble.

## THE CHALLENGE

As hard as it may seem, humility is possible for teens. It really is rather simple. Start by understanding that you are gifted by God. Know what your talents are and then think about how you can use those gifts and talents for service and sacrifice. You can do this service and sacrifice for your parish community, and school. This is what God's Word in James was saying (James 3:13) to show your works by a good life. This is the real challenge for the teen today. You are called to live a good life. The best part is that you can do that. You can live a good life with virtue. Notice that the book of Sirach tells you that by this good life of humility you "will find favor with God." What more could you ask from God? With His favor you can bring many of your fellow students to also receive His favor. Think this week of ways that you can cultivate this virtue of radical humility. Remember it must be radical and not just humility. It must be radical so that it is hard and durable against all who would tear you down.

#77: **Ir** = Iridium = **Ir**reproachable

## THE CALL

Meet the most corrosive resistant element there is. It is Iridium. It is not even affected by air, water and acids. This is one stable element. It was even used in combination with another element to make the official meter bar. It stabilizes the method of measuring in meters. A rather irreproachable event.

Being irreproachable is a great attribute of our God. He is such a power and strength for you that He, being one who is blameless and faultless, is a source of stability for you. A true tower of strength and power in a world filled with weakness and lack of direction. In these days you do not use the word irreproachable so much, but rather speak of a person as being blameless or faultless. Thus that which is irreproachable is also blameless and faultless. What an unique way to also think of the Lord.

THE WORD OF GOD SAYS...

Colossians 1:22 (NRSV)
22 he has now reconciled in his fleshly body through death, so as to present you holy and blameless and irreproachable before him—

1 Thessalonians 5:23 (NAB)
23 May the God of peace make you perfect in holiness. May he preserve you whole and entire, spirit, soul, and body, irreproachable at the coming of our Lord Jesus Christ.

1 Corinthians 1:7–8 (NAB)
7 so that you are not lacking in any spiritual gift as you wait for the revelation of our Lord Jesus Christ. 8 He will keep you firm to the end, irreproachable on the day of our Lord Jesus (Christ).

Hebrews 7:26 (RSV)

[26] For it was fitting that we should have such a high priest, holy, blameless, unstained, separated from sinners, exalted above the heavens.

Psalm 19:13 (RSV)

[13] Keep back thy servant also from presumptuous sins; let them not have dominion over me! Then I shall be blameless, and innocent of great transgression.

Proverbs 28:10 (RSV)

[10] He who misleads the upright into an evil way will fall into his own pit; but the blameless will have a goodly inheritance.

1 Thessalonians 2:10 (RSV)

[10] You are witnesses, and God also, how holy and righteous and blameless was our behavior to you believers.

THE CHALLENGE:

You need an irreproachable God who is concerned for and about you. He gives the model and example of being irreproachable, that is, blameless. As God is blameless, faultless and innocent, you need to seek those virtues as well. This will allow you to know how the Lord is concerned about you. He wants to be a force for you to be able to fight the influence of the devil in your life and lead you to a life of goodness and away from sinfulness. Think of this, when you imitate the Lord in His irreproachableness you then live a life that reflects that to your peers. How blessed is that? If you become an irreproachable, blameless and faultless, follower of the Lord you will have discovered the way to overcome sin. As sin is a great evil in one's life, so is the Lord's irreproachableness the example of the greatest mercy for you. Plan today to be an irreproachable man or woman of God by standing for a truth of faith that someone in your class may be making fun of that you believe. In other words, hold your ground, be irreproachable, be blameless, and you will be blessed this day.

# 6

## THE JOURNEY THROUGH THE FINAL FAMILIES OF TRANSITIONAL METALS FROM GROUPS 10, 11, 12 AND THE VIRTUES ASSOCIATED WITH THEIR SYMBOLS

This large family of Transitional Metals concludes with the elements of groups 10, 11, and 12. There is nothing lost of what this final grouping of transitional metals contains. There is also an incredible list of virtues associated with the symbols of these elements. Consider them now for strength on your journey to holiness.

CHEMICAL ELEMENT:    SPIRITUAL ELEMENT OF VIRTUE:

Number: Name: Symbol

GROUP 10:

| Number: Name | Symbol | Virtue |
|---|---|---|
| 28 Nickel | Ni | **Ni**ce |
| 46 Palladium | Pd | **Pd**-in-full |
| 78 Platinum | Pt | **P**rayer **t**ime |

GROUP 11:

| 29 Copper | Cu | **Cu**ltivate the faith |
|-----------|----|-----------|
| 47 Silver | Ag | **Ag**reeable |
| 79 Gold | Au | **Au**thentic |

GROUP 12:

| 30 Zinc | Zn | **Z**ealous **n**ature |
|---------|----|-----------|
| 48 Cadmium | Cd | **C**hrist **d**oer |
| 80 Mercury | Hg | **H**oly **g**uidelines |

GROUP 10:
#28: **Ni** = Nickel = **Ni**ce

## THE CALL

When you hear nickel you think of the coin (which interestingly only contains one-quarter of the element nickel). Stainless steel is the application in which most nickel is used. You probably have a nice stove or sink made out of stainless steel. Nickel steel is also used for burglar-proof vaults and armour plate like that used for the Pope mobile. You like nickel in your NiCd (nickel-cadmium) rechargeable batteries. It is clear to see that nickel does some very nice things for people. When you think of NICE, you may have a variety of definitions that come to mind. Webster's has as one of its definitions "properly modest, well-mannered." This certainly is a great expression of a virtue for a teen. Another way to be nice is to be admirable. It also expresses a need that seems to be "lost virtue" for teens today. The reputation is that teens are anything but admirable modest and well-mannered. But with a desire to build trust a teen can do many nice, considerate and admirable things. Read how God sees being nice and admirable.

## THE WORD OF GOD SAYS...

Jeremiah 12:6 (RSV)
[6] For even your brothers and the house of your father, even they have dealt treacherously with you; they are in full cry after you; believe them not, though they speak fair words to you."

Philippians 4:8-9 (NIV)
[8] Finally, brothers and sisters, whatever is true, whatever is noble, whatever is right, whatever is pure, whatever is lovely, whatever is admirable—if anything is excellent or praiseworthy—think about such things. [9] Whatever you have learned or received or heard from me, or seen in me—put it into practice. And the God of peace will be with you.

2 Maccabees 7:20 (RSV)
[20] The mother was especially admirable and worthy of honorable memory. Though she saw her seven sons perish within a single day, she bore it with good courage because of her hope in the Lord.

Titus 3: 1-2 ((NIV)
[1] Remind the people to be subject to rulers and authorities, to be obedient, to be ready to do whatever is good, [2] to slander no one, to be peaceable and considerate, and always to be gentle toward everyone.

James 3:17-18 (NIV)
[17] But the wisdom that comes from heaven is first of all pure; then peace-loving, considerate, submissive, full of mercy and good fruit, impartial and sincere. [18] Peacemakers who sow in peace reap a harvest of righteousness.

## THE CHALLENGE

"A child's prayer: "Dear God, make all the bad people good, and make all the good people nice.""[5]

" Be kind to people until you make your first million. After that people will be nice to you." [6]

These are interesting epigrams. It makes you think how do people really understand being nice. The world seems to say that you have to have something to be seen by others as being nice or considerate . This is not the way the Lord wishes to have you look at being nice. Try looking again at Webster's definition. Now is the time for teens to try to be properly modest and well mannered. It amazes me that one of the big summer events for many teens is to be enrolled in programs of etiquette to teach them to be modest and well mannered. Strange that this now needs to be taught. Teens need to learn these things by observing their elders. It also gives us a moment to pause and think of other important times when one should be modest, considerate and well-mannered, and that is your behavior in Church. Too often many teens come to the great celebration of the mystery of the Eucharist as though it were just another social occasion for them. It would be interesting to have you as a teen come very properly dressed to church on Sunday and make a great witness to all there. Can you see it. The questions will come, "why are you dressed up?" Will your answer be "I am here to participate in the great gift of Jesus of Himself to us in this miracle of the Eucharist". Think of the impact on your

5    Tan, P. L. (1996, c1979). *Encyclopedia of 7700 illustrations.* Garland TX: Bible Communications.
6    Tan, P. L. (1996, c1979). *Encyclopedia of 7700 illustrations* . Garland TX: Bible Communications.

peers and on the adults. Let this be a task of yours for the coming Sunday. No need to have anyone urge you to do this, just decide to do it yourself.

#46: **Pd** = Palladium = "**Pd**-in-full"

THE CALL

If you have a really fine watch it probably has parts made with the metal palladium. It is also known as "white gold." Therefore, that gives it a category of being something precious. Many wrist watches have palladium in them. It will take a good amount of money to pay for one of these watches. It will be yours when it is paid-in-full. If you have "Pd in full" on a bill you have a fine situation. It gives you a sense of relief. The debt is over. It is a fine-tuning of your money situation. We all love to see the abbreviation "Pd". It marks a completion of an event in one's life. We all have had the benefit of Jesus marking "Pd" on the bill of our life. He paid for our sins and brought us the gift of salvation and redemption by His death on the cross.

THE WORD OF GOD SAYS...

Leviticus 25:51 (RSV)
[51] If there are still many years, according to them he shall refund out of the price paid for him the price for his redemption.

Matthew 18:34–35 (NJB)
[34] And in his anger the master handed him over to the torturers till he should pay all his debt. [35] And that is how my heavenly Father will deal with you unless you each forgive your brother from your heart.'

Luke 12:58–59 (NJB)
⁵⁸ For example: when you are going to court with your opponent, make an effort to settle with him on the way, or he may
drag you before the judge and the judge hand you over to the
officer and the officer have you thrown into prison. ⁵⁹ I tell you,
you will not get out till you have paid the very last penny.'

Hebrews 2:17 (NIV84)
¹⁷ For this reason he had to be made like his brothers in every
way, in order that he might become a merciful and faithful
high priest in service to God, and that he might make atonement for the sins of the people.

## THE CHALLENGE

It is not comfortable to have a debt is it? Think of it. Do you
have any debts right now? Do you owe your parents for your car?
How about the iPad you just bought, not the low-end version
but the one with the bigger memory? Who do you owe for that?
Or the new flat screen TV you wanted for your room. What did
you say to the person, who loaned you the money, about when
and how you would pay it back? It is not difficult to take care of
one debt, let alone several of them. Now think about the debt
all of us owed for the sinful nature we inherited at our birth. As
our Church teaches we all were born with original sin and need
that removed by the grace of baptism so that we can have membership with the Lord. As Luke said in the scriptures (above) no
departing until you have paid the very last mite. There is that
"Pd" word again. Yes, Jesus did it! He paid the whole debt for all
of us. He atoned for our debt. Atonement means the debt is "pd-
in-full." No one was left out. Now it is your turn to consider how
you can mark "Pd" on someone's debt to you. It is not an easy

task, but look at who is in debt to you. What can you forgive? It may only be a part of the debt, but it would be a great feeling of kindness to that person if you were to do it. The other side of the coin is that if you have a debt with someone. See what you can do to get it marked "Pd" sooner than expected. If you did, you would be acting in the model of Jesus.

#78: **Pt** = Platinum = **P**rayer **t**ime

## THE CALL

You all know about platinum. It is as resistant as gold to corrosion and tarnishing. Platinum has many uses, but as you know it is most often used in jewelry because of its ability to resist corrosion and tarnishing. Maybe you even have a ring or piece of jewelry made with platinum. It has a symbol of Pt, and for us this leads us to think of Prayer Time.

It too will protect you from corrosion and tarnishing of your faith and the work of the evil one in your life.

## THE WORD OF GOD SAYS:

Psalm 31:6 (RSV)
[6] For this shall every one that is holy pray to thee in a seasonable time. And yet in a flood of many waters, they shall not come nigh unto him.

Psalm 68:14 (RSV)
[14] But as for me, my prayer is to thee, O Lord; for the time of thy good pleasure, O God. In the multitude of thy mercy hear me, in the truth of thy salvation.

Ephesians 6:18 (RSV)
[18] By all prayer and supplication praying at all times in the spirit: and in the same watching with all instance and supplication for all the saints.

## THE CHALLENGE

St. Paul gives us great direction that we should be praying at all times in the Spirit. This translates for young people, in being aware of your need to pray so that you will have a focus on the Lord and that in all difficulties the Lord will be your strength. Prayer time is also most important for a young person who is afflicted with so many anxieties and confrontations. Prayer time gives you a chance to step aside from all of the pressures created by your peers, stop and listen, in a quiet place, to what the Lord wants to tell you. Let prayer be your platinum time, that is, it prepares you not to be tarnished, or have your great gift of faith tarnished. Today do a "platinum" thing. Try to establish a prayer time every day, even if it is only a few minutes. Before you have dinner tonight go to your room and be quiet for a 10-minute prayer time. During this time listen as the Lord is listening to you and hear His movement in your heart. Then go with peace in your heart to share a meal with your family. Maybe you should also lead the prayers before meals with your family.

## GROUP 11:

#29: **Cu** = Copper = **Cu**ltivate the faith

## THE CALL

Cultivating the faith is a real challenge for every teen. This is a necessary first step before one can be an evangelizer. It is a precursor that you need to do to be sure that you have a grasp on the faith. You need to check what you know about the truths of faith. Copper is a trace element that is essential in just small quantities in the human body, but without it many body reactions cannot take place. But note it is just a small amount, a precursor to have other things happen. We know that copper is used in coins, namely the penny. Pennies build into nickels, dimes, etc., small but a builder to bigger things. This is what you need to cultivate the faith. Cultivate the faith and it grows in ways you will never expect because you are growing as well. God teaches you how to cultivate the faith. Read His word now.

## THE WORD OF GOD SAYS...

Hebrews 6:7–8 (RSV)
[7] For land which has drunk the rain that often falls upon it, and brings forth vegetation useful to those for whose sake it is cultivated, receives a blessing from God. [8] But if it bears thorns and thistles, it is worthless and near to being cursed; its end is to be burned.

Proverbs 28:19 (NAB)
[19] He who cultivates his land will have plenty of food, but from idle pursuits a man has his fill of poverty.

James 3:18 (NAB)
[18] And the fruit of righteousness is sown in peace for those who cultivate peace.

Psalm 37: 3-4 (NASB)
[3] Trust in the Lord and do good; Dwell in the land and cultivate faithfulness. [4] Delight yourself in the Lord; And He will give you the desires of your heart.

## THE CHALLENGE

When it comes to cultivating the faith, you need to devote your time and thought to foster the beauty of the Church. A good place to start is the Catechism of the Catholic Church. This is a treasure chest of knowledge in brief form, and not in complicated language either. Now teens have a special edition of the Catechism called the YOUCAT. It makes it even easier to read and learn.

A great way to cultivate the faith is to ask yourself some basic questions. What are the things that I struggle with or may even have doubts about the faith. Seek the answers to these questions through study. This will help you to be prepared when your peers ask those same questions. Make this a project that you will be involved in just for a couple of hours each week. Watch what a resource of information you have at the end of just one month.

We can see from God's word above that He expects us to do the task of cultivating the faith so that we can pass it on. This passing on of the faith for Catholics is known as tradition. This is how the faith preached by the Lord was first transmitted to the early Christians before the Bible became a reality. Now it is your chance to continue the gift of tradition of faith by passing it on. Do it after you cultivate the faith.

#47: **Ag** = Silver = **Ag**reeable

## THE CALL

Finally, we are at an element that you are familiar with. Silver is well-known to everyone. Your mom probably has a set of sterling silver eating utensils. You probably only use them for special occasions like the holidays. The sterling silver is so valued because of its beautiful appearance. Maybe you need to use this quality of sterling silver, which is to be brilliant, to reflect that you are Agreeable. To be agreeable means one is pleased and ready to consent to what is asked of one. The Lord is always asking you to be a saint. Will you be agreeable. God's word gives you some hints.

## THE WORD OF GOD SAYS...

Matthew 18:19 (RSV)
[19] Again I say to you, if two of you agree on earth about anything they ask, it will be done for them by my Father in heaven.

Job 6:25 (NAB)
[25] How agreeable are honest words; yet how unconvincing is your argument!

Matthew 5:25 (NKJV)
[25] Agree with your adversary quickly, while you are on the way with him, lest your adversary deliver you to the judge, the judge hand you over to the officer, and you be thrown into prison.

2 Corinthians 13:11 (RSV)
[11] Finally, brethren, farewell. Mend your ways, heed my appeal,

agree with one another, live in peace, and the God of love and peace will be with you.

1 Timothy 6:3–5 (RSV)

[3] If any one teaches otherwise and does not agree with the sound words of our Lord Jesus Christ and the teaching which accords with godliness, [4] he is puffed up with conceit, he knows nothing; he has a morbid craving for controversy and for disputes about words, which produce envy, dissension, slander, base suspicions, [5] and wrangling among men who are depraved in mind and bereft of the truth, imagining that godliness is a means of gain.

## THE CHALLENGE

It is hard to be agreeable isn't it? It means that, when you think you know it all and someone else may have a better idea. Then you have to be agreeable to that idea. You do not want to do that. It touches at your pride to admit that someone else has a better idea. But this is the real stuff of being agreeable. You must always be agreeable with the "sound word of Our Lord Jesus Christ." If you are not, the bible tells you that you are "conceited, understanding nothing , and have a morbid disposition". These are not attitudes you want to be known for. Who wants to be known as conceited among their peers? If you are conceited, you will not have many friends. On the other hand, if you develop the virtue of being agreeable, you will "encourage one another…and the God of love and peace will be with you." Now comes the challenge for you. Seek to be really agreeable with your parents one day this week. Seek to do something that you would not normally do if they ask you. Also try a really high bar, be agreeable with a brother or sister or classmate at least one day this week.

#79: **Au** = Gold = **Au**thentic

## THE CALL:

You are as "good as gold" is a saying you have no doubt heard. Gold is a well-known metal of yellow color. It is the most malleable and ductile metal. A great "gee whiz "fact about gold is that one ounce of gold can be beaten out to 300 square feet. That is why it is often used to gold leaf domes on important buildings. Perhaps you have seen the famous golden dome of the University of Notre Dame as an example of this gold leafing. It is a good conductor of heat and electricity, and is unaffected by air and most chemical solutions. It is also well known as a currency in many countries such as the United States. When something is made of gold it is known to be authentic. That is why we have chosen to remember the virtue of "Au" as authentic. When a follower of the Lord is faithful to Him and His commandments, they are truly an authentic Christian.

## THE WORD:

Isaiah 13:12 (D-R)
[12] A man shall be more precious than gold, yea a man than the finest of gold.

1 Peter 1:7–9 (D-R)
[7] That the trial of your faith (much more precious than gold, which is tried by the fire) may be found unto praise and glory and honor at the appearing of Jesus Christ. [8] Whom having not seen, you love: in whom also now though you see him not, you believe and, believing, shall rejoice with joy unspeakable and glorified;

[9] Receiving the end of your faith, even the salvation of your souls.

## THE CHALLENGE:

Jesus always presented an authentic image of His Father. He did all things as if they were purified gold, which we read in the scriptures. Young people today have to live a truly authentic life in conformity with the Lord. If you do, you will be recognized as a person worth one's weight in gold. To be authentic is to be respected by one's peers. If one is authentic, then one has the value of gold in one's life. How can you live this golden life? It is not difficult. It means that one has to be consistent in good choices. Golden, as being a witness of the values of Jesus in your life. A golden example, if you will. If you authentically live the message of the scriptures, you live on a golden path to be with the Lord. If you are living the golden rule, you are an authentic person. If you would simply think in the next few days to choose to be, a person who is making authentic, gold like, decisions, you will be that faithful person. Do something very simple to help an older person in your neighborhood so that they can have a sense of value. Go to visit them or offer to clean their yard or house. Take the opportunity to authentically reflect the golden image of God to them. Then be blessed by seeing how you have blessed their life. You will experience also a blessing for being kind to another person in the imitation of Jesus.

## GROUP 12

#30: **Zn** = Zinc = **Z**ealous **n**ature

## THE CALL

A zealous nature is a virtue that is well spoken in the Scriptures. It is an important virtue for the life of faith. Not too unlike the importance of zealousness in your faith, is zinc in nature. It is an important component of the protein insulin, which is responsible for the metabolism of sugars in your bodies. The result of that metabolism is that glucose releases energy for your bodies to function. Energy function is what a person with a zealous nature also has.

## THE WORD OF GOD SAYS...

Acts 21:20 (RSV)
[20] And when they heard it, they glorified God. And they said to him, "You see, brother, how many thousands there are among the Jews of those who have believed; they are all zealous for the law.

Acts 22:3 (RSV)
[3] "I am a Jew, born at Tarsus in Cilicia, but brought up in this city at the feet of Gamaliel, educated according to the strict manner of the law of our fathers, being zealous for God as you all are this day.

Titus 2:11–14 (RSV)
[11] For the grace of God has appeared for the salvation of all men, [12] training us to renounce irreligion and worldly passions, and to live sober, upright, and godly lives in this world, [13] awaiting our blessed hope, the appearing of the glory of our great God and Savior Jesus Christ, [14] who gave himself for us to redeem us from all iniquity and to purify for himself a people of his own who are zealous for good deeds.

1 Peter 3:13 (RSV)
[13] Now who is there to harm you if you are zealous for what is right?

2 Peter 1:10–11 (RSV)
[10] Therefore, brethren, be the more zealous to confirm your call and election, for if you do this you will never fall; [11] so there will be richly provided for you an entrance into the eternal kingdom of our Lord and Savior Jesus Christ.

2 Peter 3:14 (RSV)
[14] Therefore, beloved, since you wait for these, be zealous to be found by him without spot or blemish, and at peace.

Sirach 27:3 (RSV)
[3] If a man is not steadfast and zealous in the fear of the Lord, his house will be quickly overthrown.

Proverbs 23:17 (NIV)
[17] Do not let your heart envy sinners, but always be zealous for the fear of the LORD.

THE CHALLENGE

Another way to look at being of a zealous nature, is to say that you go about the living of your faith with great enthusiasm. You know what enthusiasm is like. Just recall what you feel like when you are at a championship game, either as a participant or an observer in the stands. Think of the energy you expend during the event. Your enthusiasm for your school is very evident and your involvement is dynamic. This is what having a zealous nature for your faith should mean to you. Put that same kind of enthusiasm into being a follower of Christ. Try thinking of that game enthusiasm this week when you come upon a fellow classmate who is doing some very immoral things. They tell you they are, for example, going to have a real time at the weekend party. Put into action your zealous nature and get them to see that this choice is not part of God's plan for them. See the scriptures above for strength in the task before you.

#48: **Cd** = Cadmium = **C**hrist **d**oer

THE CALL

What is a Christ doer? That person is a true disciple of Christ. He is one who follows the living Christ and is a doer of what the Lord asks. Cadmium is much like a disciple in the world of nature. Cadmium is used to protect other metals. You probably have cadmium that you use all the time. If you have a Ni-Cd battery you have cadmium in your possession. You see how it then becomes a doer, giving power from its source. That is your call to give power from your source Jesus. Let us verify that with what God has to say.

THE WORD OF GOD SAYS...

James 1:22–25 (RSV)
[22] But be doers of the word, and not hearers only, deceiving yourselves. [23] For if any one is a hearer of the word and not a doer, he is like a man who observes his natural face in a mirror; [24] for he observes himself and goes away and at once forgets what he was like. [25] But he who looks into the perfect law, the law of liberty, and perseveres, being no hearer that forgets but a doer that acts, he shall be blessed in his doing.

Romans 2:13 (RSV)
[13] For it is not the hearers of the law who are righteous before God, but the doers of the law who will be justified.

## THE CHALLENGE

Do you feel you have a handle on the truth? This is a great search for most teens. If you search, and you have truth in hand, then you need to be able to do something with that truth. That doing is what Christ wants of you. He wants you to be able to be a disciple of the truth and share it with others. That is what the bible tells us in James' statement that you be "doers of the word." That is a great task. If you do, you will earn the respect of your peers and many adults as well. Select an action that will require a sacrifice from you this week, such as taking some of your clothes and food to a homeless shelter. Even use some of your allowance for the week to buy some food to bring. This is how it works. Make a decision, and follow through with that decision. Then you are a doer. But note that the Lord is asking that you be doers of the word of God. This gives you another challenge. That is to read the word of God to know what to do. Spend ten minutes a day reading the Bible, listen to what is being said to you. Make a decision to do what the word of God asks. Then you can be a certified "doer of the word." Remember it is doers, who with God's help, turn dreams into realities.

#80: **Hg** = Mercury = **H**oly **g**uidelines

## THE CALL

Most of you have had some type of science and know well the element mercury. Even if you have not had any science you have seen mercury used around you. It is well known that mercury is the only common metal that is a liquid at the ordinary temperatures. It also is called quicksilver. And you thought that quicksilver was only a brand of sportswear. Mercury is also known for its use in thermometers. Because it has a high rate of heat expansion it is fairly constant over a large range of temperatures. That is why it is so accurate in being able to tell temperatures.

This ability to tell temperatures so carefully is why we can say that its scientific symbol Hg, can help us understand a spiritual gift for our lives. Let the H represent "Holy" and the "g" represent "guidance." Holy guidance suggests to us the way that God gives us guidance is through His commandments. These are really the guidance we need in our lives to make us holy. Note that, as mercury can be constant and accurate, so the commandments are constant and accurate in giving us Holy guidance.

THE WORD OF GOD SAYS:

Proverbs 11:14 (RSV)
[14] Where there is no guidance, a people falls; but in an abundance of counselors there is safety.

4 Maccabees 14:6 (RSV)
[6] Just as the hands and feet are moved in harmony with the guidance of the mind, so those holy youths, as though moved by an immortal spirit of devotion, agreed to go to death for its sake.

Hebrews 12:14–17 (RSV)
[14] Strive for peace with all men, and for the holiness without which no one will see the Lord. [15] See to it that no one fail to obtain the grace of God; that no "root of bitterness" spring up and cause trouble, and by it the many become defiled; [16] that

no one be immoral or irreligious like Esau, who sold his birthright for a single meal. [17] For you know that afterward, when he desired to inherit the blessing, he was rejected, for he found no chance to repent, though he sought it with tears.

1 Thessalonians 4:1–4 (RSV)
[1] Finally, brethren, we beseech and exhort you in the Lord Jesus, that as you learned from us how you ought to live and to please God, just as you are doing, you do so more and more. [2] For you know what instructions we gave you through the Lord Jesus. [3] For this is the will of God, your sanctification: that you abstain from unchastity; [4] that each one of you know how to take a wife for himself in holiness and honor,

1 Peter 1:14–17 (RSV)
[14] As obedient children, do not be conformed to the passions of your former ignorance, [15] but as he who called you is holy, be holy yourselves in all your conduct; [16] since it is written, "You shall be holy, for I am holy." [17] And if you invoke as Father him who judges each one impartially according to his deeds, conduct yourselves with fear throughout the time of your exile.

1 Corinthians 12:28 (NIV)
[28] And God has placed in the church first of all apostles, second prophets, third teachers, then miracles, then gifts of healing, of helping, of guidance, and of different kinds of tongues.

THE CHALLENGE

When you want Holy guidance, you need to listen to the truths of the God's word and how that holy Word is taught to you and the guidance you receive from the Church's teaching authority.

One of the real ways this comes to you is how the Church is faithful to God's Word. That faithfulness leads you in a holy way. This is seen clearly in the way that it helps you to form your conscience to be faithful to what God expects of you. The scriptures say, "If you love me, keep my commandments." The Ten Commandments then provide that guidance and a way to form your conscience. Challenge yourself to study these commandments and help them give you a very clear way to lead a holy life. Why not spend some time each day for the next 10 days to read and study one commandment each day.

If you can, study just one commandment each day. Then list one thing each commandment teaches you on that day. This is how God gives you holy guidance to have a straight path to holiness. The end result of these 10 days will be a great list of how God gives you the way to judge the right way to live. This is a real guarantee to holy guidance and how you can be a guide to your peers.

# 7

## MEET THE MEMBERS OF GROUP 13 THE BORON FAMILY AND THE VIRTUES RELATED TO THEIR SYMBOLS

Now we meet the five members of the Boron family. Some of these elements are familiar and others not. But all of the virtues related to their symbols are mighty virtues for teens to live.

CHEMICAL ELEMENT:    SPIRITUAL ELEMENT OF VIRTUE:

Number: Name: Symbol

GROUP 13: BORON FAMILY

| | | |
|---|---|---|
| 5 Boron | B | **B**lessings |
| 13 Aluminum | Al | **Al**mighty God |
| 31 Gallium | Ga | **Ga**llant |
| 49 Indium | In | **In**dwelling of the Holy Spirit |
| 81 Thallium | Tl | **T**enacious **L**iving |

## #5: **B** = Boron = **B**lessings

## THE CALL

Each of us has blessings in our lives. A book on blessings tells us how children should seek the blessing of their parents each time they leave the house. It is kind of like Boron, which is a close relative of Borax, a famous cleaning substance from the desserts of California. Boron is known for its cleaning properties. That is what blessings do in your life. If you are "clean inside" you are worthy of the blessings of God.

## THE WORD OF GOD SAYS...

Psalm 144:15 (RSV)
<sup>15</sup> Happy the people to whom such blessings fall! Happy the people whose God is the LORD!

Proverbs 10:6 (RSV)
<sup>6</sup> Blessings are on the head of the righteous, but the mouth of the wicked conceals violence.

1 Corinthians 9:23 (RSV)
<sup>23</sup> I do it all for the sake of the gospel, that I may share in its blessings.

Sirach 40:17 (RSV)
<sup>17</sup> Kindness is like a garden of blessings, and almsgiving endures for ever.

## THE CHALLENGE

Seek from your parents their blessings in all that you do. This keeps you accountable, and responsible and in so doing really gives you freedom. You are able to do things then that have a value and hold purpose. Your also free your parents from worry, and you don't cheat them of being proud of you as their child. They do not have to make excuses for bad behavior, because you are seeking their blessings in all that you do. This is the harvest of blessings that God's word promises to you. By sharing blessings you enlarge your parent's hearts and your own. It will also deepen your commitment to your parents and their commitment to you and all of you to the Lord. That alone is a blessing. Therefore, sometime this week go to one or both of your parents and ask them for a blessing before you go to school or before an athletic event. Watch their reaction, and then give thanks to God.

#13: **Al** = Aluminum = **Al**mighty God

## THE CALL

Jesus is the Almighty God. Recognize Jesus and then you can say you have seen the Almighty God and the True Son of God. Aluminum in nature is a soft metal and does not have much strength alone, but when it is combined with other elements it becomes strong. This is the call to each of you, alone you may be shiny but not much strength, all you have to do is join yourself and your life's direction with the Lord and his plan for your life and then you will have great strength. Do not forget He is the Almighty God.

## THE WORD OF GOD SAYS...

Genesis 17:1 (RSV)
[1] When Abram was ninety-nine years old the LORD appeared to Abram, and said to him, "I am God Almighty; walk before me, and be blameless.

Sirach 50:17 (RSV)
[17] Then all the people together made haste and fell to the ground upon their faces to worship their Lord, the Almighty, God Most High.

Revelation 11:17 (RSV)
[17] "We give thanks to thee, Lord God Almighty, who art and who wast, that thou hast taken thy great power and begun to reign.

Psalm 91:1–2 (RSV)
[1] He who dwells in the shelter of the Most High, who abides in the shadow of the Almighty, [2] will say to the LORD, "My refuge and my fortress; my God, in whom I trust."

Job 11:7 (RSV)
[7] "Can you find out the deep things of God?
Can you find out the limit of the Almighty?

## THE CHALLENGE

A great worship song is titled Almighty. It gives this great message: "Almighty, most holy God, Faithful through the ages, Almighty, most holy Lord, Glorious, almighty God."

Now is the time for young people to come together in a mighty group to seek the Almighty God. You can do it very simply by making a commitment to gather with your peers regularly for fellowship at your church youth group. Learn the incredible blessing that comes from taking time on a regular basis to gather for a time of worshiping God especially in music and prayer. Couple this time of praise and worship with some time in adoration of the Lord in the Blessed Sacrament. Then you too will know that Jesus is the Almighty God.

#31: **Ga** = Gallium = **Ga**llant

THE CALL

Gallant in Webster's Dictionary lists, as one of the meanings, to be " noble in bearing or spirit, brave." When I hear this I think of the movie Brave Heart. Gallium when painted on glass gives it a mirror surface. Therefore, it helps you to see yourself as you are. What an insight. Pray God you see yourself as having a brave heart for the Lord. Pray God that you are a person of noble spirit. Pray that you are a gallant teen for Christ.

THE WORD OF GOD SAYS...

Sirach 19:10 (RSV)
[10] Have you heard a word? Let it die with you.
Be brave! It will not make you burst!

Isaiah 33:7 (NIV)
[7] Look, their brave men cry aloud in the streets; the envoys of peace weep bitterly.

Tobit 7:18 (RSV)
[18] "Be brave, my child; the Lord of heaven and earth grant you joy in place of this sorrow of yours. Be brave, my daughter."

1 Chronicles 12:21 (NIV)
[21] They helped David against raiding bands, for all of them were brave warriors, and they were commanders in his army.

THE CHALLENGE

Be a mirror image of God. Be His "brave hearted" followers. Be His followers who are noble of heart and spirit. Be a gallant teen for the Lord. This should be an easy one for teens to live. Be so strong of heart and gallant (brave) that no one can fault your example. Do the brave hearted thing when asked to help someone in need. You can do this easily, for example, see how you can be of help to the religious education program in your parish. Maybe you could assist teaching some of the younger children. How great would that be. How brave that would be. Think of the effect of a teen, alive with the faith, coming to teach younger children. They would have such attention and be so impressed. You can give them excitement about their faith because they will see it in you. But it takes a gallant person, a brave person, to do that. Do you think that you could be that brave hearted person?

#49: **In** = Indium = **In**dwelling of the Holy Spirit

THE CALL

Indium as an element is used as a backing to glass to make it into a mirror. It is said that using indium makes a better mirror than those made with silver. The same is true of the Indwelling of the Holy Spirit. With the Holy Spirit's presence in you, you can reflect a mirror image of what it means to be created in the image and likeness of God. What a great gift has been given to you by this Indwelling which began at Baptism.

THE WORD OF GOD SAYS...

John 14:16–17 (RSV)
[16] And I will pray the Father, and he will give you another Counselor, to be with you for ever, [17] even the Spirit of truth, whom the world cannot receive, because it neither sees him nor knows him; you know him, for he dwells with you, and will be in you.

John 15:4 (RSV)
[4] Abide in me, and I in you. As the branch cannot bear fruit by itself, unless it abides in the vine, neither can you, unless you abide in me.

Romans 8:9 (RSV)
[9] But you are not in the flesh, you are in the Spirit, if in fact the Spirit of God dwells in you. Any one who does not have the Spirit of Christ does not belong to him.

1 Corinthians 6:19–20 (RSV)
[19] Do you not know that your body is a temple of the Holy Spirit within you, which you have from God? You are not your own; [20] you were bought with a price. So glorify God in your body.

Ephesians 4:22–24 (RSV)

²² Put off your old nature which belongs to your former manner of life and is corrupt through deceitful lusts, ²³ and be renewed in the spirit of your minds, ²⁴ and put on the new nature, created after the likeness of God in true righteousness and holiness.

## THE CHALLENGE

Pope John Paul II wrote ( Novo millennio ineunte) " since Baptism is a true entry into the holiness of God through incorporation into Christ and the indwelling of his Spirit, it would be a contradiction to settle for a life of mediocrity, marked by a minimalist ethic and a shallow religiosity." This gives you the importance of the Indwelling of the Holy Spirit. Certainly as a teen you do not want to be known as someone who settles for a life of mediocrity. How would that play out if you were on the varsity football team or the volley ball team? Can you picture yourself just doing the minimum and not really striving to be a winner? The same is true with what the indwelling of the Holy Spirit is all about. This is the time to stand up and accept the challenge of the Holy Spirit within you. Set yourself on track to try to pray for a powerful release of the Gifts of the Holy Spirit in your life. This is the high standard that God wants for you. He does not want you at a minimum level of faith or one that is shallow. This Indwelling of the Holy Spirit is a central means to be holy. Actually what this means is living this Indwelling of the Holy Spirit. This is what makes you a living saint. Go for it! Be a saint. Resolve today that you are going to do all you can to be free of sin. Especially make a commitment to free yourself of any addiction, if you have one, to sex, pornography, alcohol, or drugs. See that you do not need them. They keep you from being a truly human person blessed by God. Do not forget, go for being a saint. Be a great mirror of the Holy Spirit in you.

#81: **Tl** = Thallium = **T**enacious **l**iving

## THE CALL

While thallium is found in nature, it is not well known, unless you are a rat, who has come into contact with thallium, as rat poison. Thallium is a very soft and malleable metal that can be cut with a knife. It is often used in making glass used for highly reflective lenses. If you were to consume thallium you would be made very sick, being tired with headaches, leg pains, sight impairment, and even a lack of an appetite. It really takes a toll on a person, that is to say, it is very tenacious on the human system. This is our connection to the Tl, the scientific abbreviation for thallium, namely "tenacious living".

Tenacious living for the follower of Christ is an important virtue. Tenacious living implies that a person is not easily pulled apart, and perseveres. The dictionary also says that tenacious means to cling to and be persistent. It further means to adhere to or to seek a value. These are great qualities for a Christian teen. Cling to and be persistent in following the Lord, and adhere to His values for your life. With this model of living, one can easily retain being a person of respect by one's peers. Doing so allows one to show the blessings of being a person who lives a tenacious life with Christ.

## THE WORD OF GOD SAYS...

Romans 12:12 (NASB95)
[12]rejoicing in hope, persevering in tribulation, devoted to prayer,

Luke 8:15 (NIV)
[15] But the seed on good soil stands for those with a noble and good heart, who hear the word, retain it, and by persevering produce a crop.

Psalm 89:2 (RSV)
[2] For thy steadfast love was established for ever, thy faithfulness is firm as the heavens.

1 Corinthians 16:13 (RSV)
[13] Be watchful, stand firm in your faith, be courageous, be strong.

Philippians 1:27 (RSV)
[27] Only let your manner of life be worthy of the gospel of Christ, so that whether I come and see you or am absent, I may hear of you that you stand firm in one spirit, with one mind striving side by side for the faith of the gospel,

2 Thessalonians 2:15 (RSV)
[15] So then, brethren, stand firm and hold to the traditions which you were taught by us, either by word of mouth or by letter.

1 Peter 5:9 (RSV)
[9] Resist him (the devil), firm in your faith, knowing that the same experience of suffering is required of your brotherhood throughout the world.

Hebrews 3:14 (RSV)
[14] For we share in Christ, if only we hold our first confidence firm to the end,

Hebrews 6:19–20 (RSV)

[19] We have this as a sure and steadfast anchor of the soul, a hope that enters into the inner shrine behind the curtain, [20] where Jesus has gone as a forerunner on our behalf, having become a high priest for ever after the order of Melchizedek.

## THE CHALLENGE

Your call is to be tenacious in your living. You need to hold on to things that are of the Lord. Much like Linus in the comic strip "Peanuts". Carl C. Williams once said that " Charles Schultz, creator of the comic strip "Peanuts" pictures one of his characters, Linus, tenaciously clinging to his security blanket. Wherever he goes or whatever he does, Linus must have his blanket. He feels insecure without it. This may be humorous, but actually all of us have to have our security blankets of one kind or another.

"The eternal God is thy refuge, and underneath are the everlasting arms." (Deut. 33:27).

How can you make the Lord your "Linus Blanket?" It is not as difficult as you might imagine because it requires that we hold to all of the truths of our faith with a tenacious spirit. This will affect how you live the faith you have been blessed with. Your task is to examine yourself this week to see how well you had a tenacious heart living the truths of faith. Make a list this week of the various important teachings of our faith that you have lived this week and even gave testimony to with your peers. For example, did you stand for observing the fourth commandment and honored your mother or your father this week? All you would have had to do was to affirm them in some fashion such as thanking them for providing for your room and board. Or, it may be more obvious for you to do some unexpected task for them. Or, you might try to honor classmates by affirming them for some gift they have. Just tell them that you appreciated their friendship and watch their reaction. You have shown by these actions that you are not fearful of your faith and are willing to hold to tenacious living to demonstrate it.

# 8

## THE FAMILY OF GROUP 14 IS THE CARBON FAMILY AND THE VIRTUES RELATED TO THEIR SYMBOLS

Carbon is known as a chemical "power broker" since so many organic compounds contain the element. It is the leader of this group. The virtues associated with the symbols of this group are also power brokers for a holy life.

GROUP 14: CARBON FAMILY

| CHEMICAL ELEMENT: | | SPIRITUAL ELEMENT OF VIRTUE: |
|---|---|---|
| Number: Name: Symbol | | |
| 6 Carbon | C | **C**atholic |
| 14 Silicon | Si | **Si**lence |
| 32 Germanium | Ge | **Ge**nerosity |
| 50 Tin | Sn | **S**teadfast **n**ature |
| 82 Lead | Pb | **P**erfect **b**ook |

#6: **C** = Carbon = **C**aring

THE CALL

Carbon is the essential element in all living things. It is the essential element that forms the basis for all organic chemistry. All living things then have carbon compounds. Being caring is an essential spiritual element for all of Christians. Our Church truly holds caring as a pride of place in the teachings of our Church. That essentially means we have the fullness of the faith that Christ wished His Church to have. One of the ways in which we share it is to care for others.

THE WORD OF GOD SAYS....

I Timothy 5:4 (NIV)
[4] But if a widow has children or grandchildren, these should learn first of all to put their religion into practice by caring for their own family and so repaying their parents and grandparents, for this is pleasing to God.

Luke 10:33–35 (RSV)
[33] But a Samaritan, as he journeyed, came to where he was; and when he saw him, he had compassion, [34] and went to him and bound up his wounds, pouring on oil and wine; then he set him on his own beast and brought him to an inn, and took care of him. [35] And the next day he took out two denarii and gave them to the innkeeper, saying, 'Take care of him; and whatever more you spend, I will repay you when I come back.'

Acts 20:28 (RSV)
[28] Take heed to yourselves and to all the flock, in which the

Holy Spirit has made you overseers, to care for the church of God which he obtained with the blood of his own Son.

1 Corinthians 12:25 (RSV)
[25] that there may be no discord in the body, but that the members may have the same care for one another.

## THE CHALLENGE

We need to understand our call as members of the Catholic Church. Being a member brings responsibilities. One of the great challenges for youth is to be able to proudly proclaim their faithfulness to the Church. Know your Church and be able to explain it to your non-Catholic peers. You are the latest in the line of disciples to continue the spread of the truths about our faith to others who really do not know or understand the great truths of our Church. One of the ways that you can demonstrate you membership in the Church is to be caring for another. You need in the next few days to do a caring act. Call one of your grandparents and tell them how proud you are of the heritage that they have given your family. They will also be blessed by your caring action. This will make you affirmed to be a CATHOLIC.

#14: **Si** = Silicon = **Si**lence

## THE CALL

Silicon is best known to you as silicon dioxide, or even more commonly as sand, from which glass is made. Our call to virtue reminds you that you need to have times of Silence. Sand on the seashore is a very peaceful image, that is also what the image, and feeling of silence should be for you. It is true that if you can be comfortable with times of silence you will develop a wonderful way to listen to the Lord in your life. There is something about silicon when it is heated and made into glass. Consider something like sand can become something through which we can see things (the glass). Silence can "be heat" in our lives and can make the silence into something that you can then see through to "see" the word of God.

## THE WORD OF GOD SAYS...

Psalm 62:1 (RSV)
[1] For God alone my soul waits in silence;
from him comes my salvation.

Ecclesiastes 3:7 (RSV)
[7] a time to rend, and a time to sew;
a time to keep silence, and a time to speak;

1 Corinthians 14:28 (RSV)
[28] But if there is no one to interpret, let each of them keep silence in church and speak to himself and to God.

Habakkuk 2:20 (RSV)
[20] But the LORD is in his holy temple;
let all the earth keep silence before him.

## THE CHALLENGE

To experience silence in a spiritual setting suggests that you really do need to be quiet. That simply means you need to stop talking once in a while. This makes it easier for one to pray, reflect, and maybe even meditate and listen to God.

Think of all the times you just talk. This often takes you away from reality and you do not even hear what others are saying. You want to be heard. If that is true for you, then you waste a lot of time. If you talk and are never silent, you cannot even hear what others are saying to you, much less what God want to say to you.

You will discover that there is a new world waiting for you when you are silent. Try just listening to a contemporary Christian song. Do not try to sing along, but attentively listen to the words. After you listen to it, pause for a few moments and then ask yourself how do these words apply to me? How will they make you a better person? How will this help you to be silent so that you hear the voice of God? If you get experience with this you will want to develop it in your life and you will also become a good listener. This will give you a new trust with your friends because they will see that you are interested in them.

#32: **Ge** = Germanium = **Ge**nerosity

THE CALL

The virtue of generosity is often spoken of in the writings of St. Paul in the New Testament. He speaks of the power of the generosity of the early Christians as being a great source of strength for him in his work for the newly growing Church. It seems that generosity reflects the ability to share what one has. Germanium is kind of a "generosity" element in nature. It gives of itself as a phosphor in fluorescent lights. These lights "glow" because of the presence of this element. The call for teens is to be a "glowing" person among their peers and elders. You can become that person by learning to be generous. The Bible tells us it is better to give than receive (Acts 20:35).

THE WORD OF GOD SAYS...

Matthew 20:15 (RSV)
[15] Am I not allowed to do what I choose with what belongs to me? Or do you begrudge my generosity?'

2 Corinthians 9:11 (RSV)
[11] You will be enriched in every way for great generosity, which through us will produce thanksgiving to God;

Romans 12:6–8 (ESV)
[6] Having gifts that differ according to the grace given to us, let us use them: if prophecy, in proportion to our faith; [7] if service, in our serving; the one who teaches, in his teaching; [8] the one who exhorts, in his exhortation; the one who contributes, in generosity; the one who leads, with zeal; the one who does acts of mercy, with cheerfulness.

2 Corinthians 9:13 (ESV)
[13] By their approval of this service, they will glorify God because of your submission that comes from your confession of the gospel of Christ, and the generosity of your contribution for them and for all others,

2 Corinthians 8:2 (NIV)
[2] In the midst of a very severe trial, their overflowing joy and their extreme poverty welled up in rich generosity.

2 Cor. 9: 11 (NRSV)
[11] You will be enriched in every way for your great generosity, which will produce thanksgiving to God through us;

Sirach 7:33 (NJB)
[33] Let your generosity extend to all the living, do not withhold it even from the dead.

Psalm 116:12-13 (NJB)
[12] What return can I make to Yahweh for his generosity to me?
[13] I shall take up the cup of salvation and call on the name of Yahweh.

## THE CHALLENGE

When the Lord gives the example (Psalm 116:12) what else can we do? Generosity asks of you to give of your gifts and resources. Teens often do not think that they can be generous since they have for too long been in a mode of receiving. Think of all of the things that you have received from your parents. Next think of how willing are you to share some of these "things" with those who do not have. This is a great experience if you will do it. Why not one day this week go through your house and see what things you really have not used much during the last year, or that you have several of the same kind of thing. For example, do you have extra soap or other toiletries? Maybe you even have some extra electronic gadgets. Take them out, do not think about it a second time, put it in a box with all that you selected that day. Now bring it to a place where the homeless gather. Your diocese probably operates one of these centers. They will welcome the things, and you will have the experience of what it feels like to be generous.

#50: **S**n = Tin = **S**teadfast **n**ature

THE CALL

If you have a Steadfast Nature you will not be a person who
does not experience any corrosion of your character. Steadfast
means you stand proudly for what you believe. Tin is that way.
Tin is used to coat other metals so that they do not corrode.
That Coke can or Pepsi can of soda you drink all the time has
tin in it so that the soda does not corrode the metal that makes
up the can.

THE WORD OF GOD SAYS...

Psalm 136:1 (RSV)
[1] O give thanks to the LORD, for he is good, for his steadfast
love endures for ever.

Sirach 5:12 (NAB)
[12] Be consistent in your thoughts; steadfast be your words.

1 Peter 5:8–9 (NAB)
[8] Be sober and vigilant. Your opponent the devil is prowling
around like a roaring lion looking for (someone) to devour. [9]
Resist him, steadfast in faith, knowing that your fellow believers throughout the world undergo the same sufferings.

Proverbs 11:19 (RSV)
[19] He who is steadfast in righteousness will live, but he who
pursues evil will die.

## THE CHALLENGE

Being of a steadfast nature is the making of a martyr. So many of the martyrs of the Church were those who were not ashamed to tell others that they were Catholic. Recall the young martyr St. Maria Goretti. She stood steadfast in keeping her virginity. She died doing this. The call to all of you today is the same. You may not be called to give up your life for the faith. But you can be a modern martyr if you have a Steadfast Nature. How does that play out for a teen today? It means that you have to be proud to be a Catholic. Many teens buy tee shirts for all kinds of occasions. Not too long ago at a conference for teens, they bought shirts that said just that, "Proud to be Catholic". Another one caught my eye as well. It read "100% Catholic." Then the real modern martyrdom comes when a teen is asked to defend his faith. It is so easy these days just to remain silent or not defend the faith with your peers. But now is the time to take up the call and be proud. Be Steadfast in your faith. Stand against the evil ones of the world that would rather not have you so strong in your faith. This is your time to show your pride. Do not only wear it on a shirt, but know it, so that you can answer questions from your peers. Make it your task to listen for a question that others challenge you on a truth of faith. Then look into the Catechism of the Catholic Church and seek out the answer. Learn it. Now you are ready to show forth that Steadfast Nature when you meet the person who asked the question. Enjoy being a modern martyr.

#82: **Pb** = Lead = **P**erfect **b**ook

## THE CALL

You have heard a lot about lead. If you drive you know that you now get unleaded gas. This is an ancient element that has many applications and it is said that it has been in use since 5000 BC. In health it is one of the most damaging elements for we humans. There are many ways we can intake it. Some is taken in even in food, or water or breathing it from the air. Probably you have heard to avoid seafood that has lead in it. Even your vegetables, meats and your soft drinks may contain some lead. The symbol for lead is Pb, and therefore, we want to make it have better applications for our journey with the Lord. Thus let Pb represent the Perfect Book, the Bible, the very word of God. This too has many applications that do not harm us but build you as sons and daughters of God. In the journey of life, it is the Perfect Book that gives us the clear and certain directions that you need to follow to have happiness in our lives.

## THE WORD OF GOD SAYS....

Psalm 19:7 (RSV)
[7] The law of the LORD is perfect, reviving the soul; the testimony of the LORD is sure, making wise the simple;

2 Timothy 3:16 (RSV)
[16] All scripture is inspired by God and profitable for teaching, for reproof, for correction, and for training in righteousness,

2 Peter 1:20–21 (RSV)
[20] First of all you must understand this, that no prophecy of

scripture is a matter of one's own interpretation, [21] because no prophecy ever came by the impulse of man, but men moved by the Holy Spirit spoke from God.

Hebrews 1:1 (RSV)
[1] In many and various ways God spoke of old to our fathers by the prophets.

1 Thessalonians 2:13 (RSV)
[13] And we also thank God constantly for this, that when you received the word of God which you heard from us, you accepted it not as the word of men but as what it really is, the word of God, which is at work in you believers.

John 6:63 (RSV)
[63] It is the spirit that gives life, the flesh is of no avail; the words that I have spoken to you are spirit and life.

THE CHALLENGE

Since the Bible is a perfect book, that makes it a very unique book. I read the following by Glenn Harris (www.shema. com). It is really interesting. Consider it now." The Bible is unique in its continuity. Imagine questioning forty different people on their religious views: people from every socioeconomic background ...(ranging from extreme poverty to immense wealth) in nearly every walk of life ...(kings and paupers, statesmen and fishermen, poets and physicians) on three separate continents ...(Asia, Africa, and Europe) in three different languages ...(Hebrew, Greek, and Aramaic) taking several forms ... (poetry, history, civil and criminal law, ethics, didactic, parable, biography, prophecy, personal correspondence ...) And spanning a period of nearly 1,500 years!"

When you are in need of a solid place to have security and truth you need go no further than the Bible. Because it is the word of God, that gives you a true basis for your morals, it is no doubt the greatest book in the world. It is your playbook for life. Do not miss its religious truth. It gives you foundations for right living in all areas of your lives. Remember since it is the perfect book of truth about God, you are really grounded if you are reading this perfect book.

You might consider a couple of interesting ways to read this perfect book. One would be to read it through from Genesis (the first book of the Bible) to Revelation (the last book).

Another way is to select a reading program that would guide you to reading the entire bible in a year. It is a great experience. Doing this will give you a great vision for a solid and good life. Try one of these suggestions for this year in your life.

# 9

## THE JOURNEY THROUGH GROUP 15
## THE NITROGEN FAMILY

The journey now continues with the group 15 family members headed by the element Nitrogen. Read the inspiring related virtues to the symbols of this family.

GROUP 15: NITROGEN FAMILY

CHEMICAL ELEMENT:               SPIRITUAL ELEMENT OF
                                VIRTUE:

Number: Name: Symbol

| 7 Nitrogen | N | **N**ear us |
| 15 Phosphorous | P | **P**rayerful |
| 33 Arsenic | As | **A**ffirming **s**pirit |
| 51 Antimony | Sb | **S**uccess **b**ound |
| 83 Bismuth | Bi | **Bi**shops |

#7: **N** = Nitrogen = **N**earness

## THE CALL

Nitrogen makes up about 78% of the atmosphere. That is amazing in percentage terms. "Nitrogen is a key component of biological molecules such as proteins (which are made from amino acids, and nucleic acids. The nitrogen cycle in nature is very important" (from web site: Web Elements) . Just as nitrogen makes important parts of our bodies, for example, muscle and DNA, so the nearness of God to us is an important element for the real "muscle" in our lives.

## THE WORD OF GOD SAYS...

Psalm 73:28 (RSV)
[28] But for me it is good to be near God; I have made the Lord GOD my refuge, that I may tell of all thy works.

Isaiah 58:2 (RSV)
[2] Yet they seek me daily, and delight to know my ways, as if they were a nation that did righteousness and did not forsake the ordinance of their God; they ask of me righteous judgments, they delight to draw near to God.

Hebrews 4:16 (RSV)
[16] Let us then with confidence draw near to the throne of grace, that we may receive mercy and find grace to help in time of need.

Deuteronomy 4:7 (RSV)
[7] For what great nation is there that has a god so near to it as the LORD our God is to us, whenever we call upon him?

James 4:8 (RSV)
[8] Draw near to God and he will draw near to you. Cleanse your hands, you sinners, and purify your hearts, you men of double mind.

Psalm 119:151 (RSV)
[151] But thou art near, O LORD, and all thy commandments are true.

THE CHALLENGE

Image the nearness of the Lord in your life. Think of Him walking by your side. What a way to keep you in the path of virtue and the nearness of His truth to be always with you. Why not try to express your nearness to someone you love. Try to replicate how God is near to you and let that person know of how you care for them. It might be that you can express it to your parents. Let them know you are grateful for them being your parents. It is a great way to develop a sense of nearness in a family that imitates the nearness of the Lord.

#15: **P** = Phosphorous = **P**rayer

THE CALL

Being prayerful is the secret to success in all that you do. Without a prayerful spirit you will not have clarity in your decisions. But by submission of all decision making, in advance to a prayerful time, will insure that you your decisions will have the blessing of God. This is no different in nature where phosphorous is an essential component to DNA. You know about DNA, the molecule of our genes that make you unique.

Science and many other areas of your lives these days use information from DNA to discover who you are. Prayerfulness discovers who you are before God. You become prayerful when you pray.

THE WORD OF GOD SAYS...

Matthew 21:22 (RSV)
[22] And whatever you ask in prayer, you will receive, if you have faith."

James 5:16 (RSV)
[16] Therefore confess your sins to one another, and pray for one another, that you may be healed. The prayer of a righteous man has great power in its effects.

Jeremiah 29:12 (RSV)
[12] Then you will call upon me and come and pray to me, and I will hear you.

Mark 11:24 (RSV)
[24] Therefore I tell you, whatever you ask in prayer, believe that you have received it, and it will be yours.

Psalm 141:2 (RSV)
[2] Let my prayer be counted as incense before thee,
and the lifting up of my hands as an evening sacrifice!

Acts 1:14 (RSV)
[14] All these with one accord devoted themselves to prayer, together with the women and Mary the mother of Jesus, and with his brothers.

Romans 12:12 (RSV)
[12] Rejoice in your hope, be patient in tribulation, be constant in prayer.

Colossians 4:2 (RSV)
[2] Continue steadfastly in prayer, being watchful in it with thanksgiving;

## THE CHALLENGE

It is not a common agenda item for teens to take time to pray. I have been so blessed with seeing a transformation that takes place with young people who have joined a missionary movement known as NET MINISTRIES. These young people give a year of their life to serve as evangelizers across the country. These young people are dedicated to developing a prayerful attitude about their lives. They take time each day for personal prayer time and for a time of team prayer. They develop a habit of prayer. This is the task of every young person. Tell yourself today that you will take some time each day for prayer. Maybe it will be as simple as reading a section of God's Word, the Bible. This is a great source of truth for your life. Check God's word above and see what happens when you do pray. (Math. 21:22)

#33: **As** = Arsenic = **A**ffirming **s**pirit

## THE CALL

You are called to have an affirming spirit. Your life must be affirming, that is, expressing in a positive way, the goodness of the Lord you have been given. Your affirming must also go out from you to others. How would you like to have the reputation that arsenic has? It is well known for its poisonous properties, but as a trace element (one that is not needed in very large amounts), it is necessary in our bodies to help prevent having your growth stunted. Being stunted is not very affirming is it? Therefore, teens need to break away from any poisonous behavior that would stunt your personalities. Having an affirming spirit is being one who allows others to grow by your affirmation of them. Check what God's word has to say.

THE WORD OF GOD SAYS...

Deut. 28:8 (NAB)
[8] The LORD will affirm his blessing upon you, on your barns and on all your undertakings, blessing you in the land that the LORD, your God, gives you.

Ephesians 4:17 (RSV)
[17] Now this I affirm and testify in the Lord, that you must no longer live as the Gentiles do, in the futility of their minds.

1 Corinthians 15:31 (NASB)
[31] I affirm, brethren, by the boasting in you which I have in Christ Jesus our Lord Jesus our Lord, I die daily.

Ephesians 4:17 (NASB)
[17] So this I say, and affirm together with the Lord, that you walk no longer just as the Gentiles also walk, in the futility of their mind.

Romans 15:8 (RSV)
[8] For I tell you that Christ became a servant to the circumcised

to show God's truthfulness, in order to confirm the promises given to the patriarchs,

Sirach 29:3 (RSV)
³ Confirm your word and keep faith with him,
and on every occasion you will find what you need.

Psalm 119:38 (ESV)
³⁸ Confirm to your servant your promise,
that you may be feared.

## THE CHALLENGE

Thinking of how the Lord affirms His blessings makes you think how you can affirm your blessings on others as well. There is another thing to think about if you have an affirming spirit. That is to look for moments for you to do some affirmation of another person. It also means to confirm others around you. You can easily do this at least once a day. Try these examples. Think of a way that you can affirm one of your parents. Maybe you can thank your mother for fixing dinner one night. Another day seek to affirm your dad for his efforts to provide for you. Think of a peer that you can affirm. Maybe one of your best friends helped you with a difficult math problem. Say something affirming. When you think about it, if you develop this affirming spirit, you will most certainly remove from your talk anything that is negative. This will also purify you from even using negative humor about another peer. This can develop a whole new feeling of excitement when you are with your friends. They will treasure your presence all the more because they know of your affirming spirit. Never forget to confirm them in their good deeds.

#51: **Sb** = Antimony = **S**uccess **b**ound

## THE CALL

Antimony is a poetic sounding word, isn't it? That may be because one of its uses in compound form is for flame-proofing. That means whatever it is applied to is insulated against defeat. Clearly then the covered substance will be success bound if it is attacked by fire. If you are one who has made a commitment to Christ, you are "flame-proofed". If you are covered or protected by the Lord, flame-proofed from the attacks of the devil, from the fires of hell then you are success bound.

## THE WORD OF GOD SAYS...

Tobit 4:6 (NAB)
6 For if you are steadfast in your service, your good works will bring success, not only to you, but also to all those who live uprightly.

Nehemiah 1:11 (RSV)
11 O Lord, let thy ear be attentive to the prayer of thy servant, and to the prayer of thy servants who delight to fear thy name; and give success to thy servant today, and grant him mercy in the sight of this man."

Sirach 11: 11 (NAB)
11 O Lord, let thy ear be attentive to the prayer of thy servant, and to the prayer of thy servants who delight to fear thy name; and give success to thy servant today, and grant him mercy in the sight of this man."

Psalms 118:25 (RSV)
²⁵ Save us, we beseech thee, O LORD! O LORD, we beseech thee, give us success!

## THE CHALLENGE

Being flame-proofed spiritually in the world today is important to the teen truly seeking to be success bound. Success as the Lord would have it. The road to real success for a teen is to do it with humility as God's Word says in Proverbs 22:4 "Humility and the fear of the Lord bring wealth and honor and life." This is how God defines success. But in order to obtain the Lord's success it must be done not only with humility but also with fear of the Lord. Fear of the Lord meaning that you understand how awesome God is. The song AWESOME GOD says it all. Our God is an awesome God. So let yourself be open to the power of that awesome God in all you do. If you have that antimonious coating and are flame-proofed then all of your success will be blessed. Do you have the courage to do as many professional athletes do when they make a great play? Notice how they are pointing up to the heavens. Let us give them the benefit of the doubt and say they are pointing to that AWESOME GOD to thank Him for the successful play. Why not take the next time you do something successfully and say to those around you, all glory to God for that success. When you have the courage to do this then you are truly SUCCESS BOUND.

#83: **Bi** = Bismuth = **Bi**shops

## THE CALL

Who ever heard of bismuth? It is not even found free in nature in the United States and so it seems a sort of mystery.

What science tells us is that bismuth is a soft, silvery metal with a bright, shiny surface and a yellowish or pinkish tinge. It is a metal type of material and can be melted and poured into molds that have the shape of letters and numbers. This is how letters were made to print newspapers until computer typesetting came along. That has largely replaced typesetting letters made of bismuth. Being poured into a mold and used to continue a message as the typesetting of old did is not too distant from what the bishops in our Church are. They are the descendants of the Apostles and therefore, they had to be molded like the Apostles to carry the message that the Apostles received from Jesus to us. This is a unique blessing to us as Church. It guarantees for us that we have the same message that Jesus gave the Apostles.

THE WORD OF GOD SAYS...

Titus 1:7–9 (RSV)
[7] For a bishop, as God's steward, must be blameless; he must not be arrogant or quick-tempered or a drunkard or violent or greedy for gain, [8] but hospitable, a lover of goodness, master of himself, upright, holy, and self-controlled; [9] he must hold firm to the sure word as taught, so that he may be able to give instruction in sound doctrine and also to confute those who contradict it.

I Timothy: 3: 1 (RSV)
[1] " The saying is sure: If any one aspires to the office of bishop, he desires a noble task."

1 Timothy 5:17–18 (RSV)
[17] Let the elders who rule well be considered worthy of double honor, especially those who labor in preaching and teaching; [18]

for the scripture says, "You shall not muzzle an ox when it is treading out the grain," and, "The laborer deserves his wages."

James 5:14–15 (RSV)
[14] Is any among you sick? Let him call for the elders of the church, and let them pray over him, anointing him with oil in the name of the Lord; [15] and the prayer of faith will save the sick man, and the Lord will raise him up; and if he has committed sins, he will be forgiven.

## THE CHALLENGE

To help us understand the role of the bishop we need to look at what the bishops of the early Church were entrusted to do. St. Ignatius of Antioch had this to say "Take care to do all things in harmony with God, with the bishop presiding in the place of God, and with the presbyters in the place of the council of the apostles.(*Letter to the Magnesians 6:1* [A.D. 110]).

"Take care, therefore, to be confirmed in the decrees of the Lord and of the apostles, in order that in everything you do, you may prosper in body and in soul, in faith and in love, in Son and in Father and in Spirit, in beginning and in end, together with your most reverend bishop; and with that fittingly woven spiritual crown, the presbytery, men of God. Be subject to the bishop and to one another as Jesus Christ was subject to the Father, and the apostles were subject to Christ and to the Father; so that there may be unity in both body and spirit" (ibid., 13:1–2).

"Indeed, when you submit to the bishop as you would to Jesus Christ, it is clear to me that you are living not in the manner of men but as Jesus Christ, who died for us, that through faith in his death you might escape dying. It is necessary, therefore— and such is your practice that you do nothing without the bishop, and that you be subject also to the presbytery, as to the apostles of Jesus Christ our hope, in whom we shall be found, if we live in him." (*Letter to the Trallians* 2:1–3 [A.D. 110]).

These are great words for you. They were written in the year 110 and give you a glimpse of the tradition and history of bishops in our Church. They also help understand the role that God has called your bishops to serve. It is also a call for you to see what you can do to support your local bishop. Think of how exciting it would be for your bishop to get a letter from you. Write to him to thank him for being a descendant of the apostles to your local Church. Also, this week make an effort everyday to say the Our Father for your local bishop. Be sure you know his name and include it in the intention of your prayer.

# 10

## THE JOURNEY CONTINUES WITH GROUP 16 THE CHALCOGENS AND THE RELATED VIRTUES TO THEIR SYMBOLS

As the journey continues through the elements we have arrived at group 16 known as the Chalcogens. If you breathe each moment then you will be introduced to the leader of the group 16 which is Oxygen. This will be an exciting journey through the virtues related to this group.

CHALCOGENS GROUP 16

| CHEMICAL ELEMENT: | | SPIRITUAL ELEMENT OF VIRTUE: |
|---|---|---|

Number: Name: Symbol

| 8 Oxygen | O | **O**bedience |
| 16 Sulfur | S | **S**tewardship |
| 34 Selenium | Se | **Se**rvant |
| 52 Tellurium | Te | **Te**mperance |
| 84 Polonium | Po | **Po**ndering |

#8: **O** = Oxygen = **O**bedience

## THE CALL

It is really hard for a young person to submit to obedience. Yet this is exactly what the Lord Himself did. Recall that He responded to obey the Blessed Mother and St. Joseph. He knew the fourth commandment, "honor your father and mother." What a great example for all of us. He was also obedient to the will of His Father to give His own life for our salvation .(John 15:10). Just as it is hard for a young person to be obedient, so your lives would find it hard to be without oxygen. It is said that your bodies are two-thirds oxygen. There are not many processes in the body that can function without oxygen. There are also not many good things that can come to a family without obedience. The same is true for your relationship with our Church. You need to be obedient to the Church.

## THE WORD OF GOD SAYS...

Romans 5:19 (RSV)
[19] For as by one man's disobedience many were made sinners, so by one man's obedience many will be made righteous.

Hebrews 5:8 (RSV)
[8] Although he was a Son, he learned obedience through what he suffered;

1 Peter 1:22 (RSV)
[22] Having purified your souls by your obedience to the truth for a sincere love of the brethren, love one another earnestly from the heart.

2 Corinthians 7:15 (RSV)
[15] And his heart goes out all the more to you, as he remembers the obedience of you all, and the fear and trembling with which you received him.

Romans 2:13 (RSV)
[13] For it is not the hearers of the law who are righteous before God, but the doers of the law who will be justified.

## THE CHALLENGE

No it is not easy to be obedient. It seems to take away your feeling of independence and freedom. But you have to look at the benefits that come from obedience. God's Word is clear that if you obey you will have a firm foundation. Recall the words of that great worship song FIRM FOUNDATION. Here they are:

Jesus You're my firm foundation, I know I can stand secure
Jesus You're my firm foundation, I put my hope in Your holy word
I put my hope in Your holy word

I have a living hope (I have a living hope)
I have a future (I have a future)
God has a plan for me (God has a plan for me)
Of this I'm sure, of this I'm sure

Your word is faithful (Your word is faithful)
Mighty with power (Mighty with power)
God will deliver me (God will deliver me)
Of this I'm sure, of this I'm sure

Jesus You're my firm foundation, I know I can stand secure
Jesus You're my firm foundation, I put my hope in Your holy
word
I put my hope in Your holy word

You're my firm foundation
You're the rock of my salvation
You're my firm foundation

*(Words & Music : Jamie Harvill & Nancy Gordon)*

But most of all the call to obedience is the way the Lord promises
us that you will be great in His kingdom. Try each day this coming week to do a clear act of obedience to one of your parents, or a
coach, or teacher. Speak to them with respect, and honor their position over you. Watch the different feeling that comes inside you.
You will discover that what appears to be a restriction on freedom
is in fact a wonderfully liberating moment. Not to say the least
that your elders' trust level in you will grow exponentially.

#16: **S** = Sulfur = **S**tewardship

THE CALL

You probably will have to ask your parents what the meaning
of stewardship means. Or you may have heard homilies in your
parish church on stewardship and know that it has something to
do with financial resources and giving to the Church. While this
is true, I would like to explore another spiritual meaning of stewardship, and that is responsibility. Sulfur is one of those elements
that you know exists without realizing it exists. This means that
you know something related to it. You can usually identify it by

its odor. Sulfur containing compounds often smell like rotten eggs. When it is there you know it, you smell it. It makes its presence known by its effect. That is the responsibility that the Lord expects of you, the stewardship of what He has given you.

## THE WORD OF GOD SAYS...

Colossians 1:25 (NASB)
<sup>25</sup> Of *this church* I was made a minister according to the stewardship from God bestowed on me for your benefit, so that I might fully carry out the *preaching of* the word of God.

1 Corinthians 9:16–17 (NASB)
<sup>16</sup> For if I preach the gospel, I have nothing to boast of, for I am under compulsion; for woe is me if I do not preach the gospel. <sup>17</sup> For if I do this voluntarily, I have a reward; but if against my will, I have a stewardship entrusted to me.

Ephesians 3:2 (NASB)
<sup>2</sup> if indeed you have heard of the stewardship of God's grace which was given to me for you.

1 Timothy 1:3–4 (ESV)
<sup>3</sup> As I urged you when I was going to Macedonia, remain at Ephesus so that you may charge certain persons not to teach any different doctrine, <sup>4</sup> nor to devote themselves to myths and endless genealogies, which promote speculations rather than the stewardship from God that is by faith.

## THE CHALLENGE

Teens have not been known to be very responsible. At least, this is the perception of modern society. When I was teaching high school students, I had the opposite experience. I found that, if the teens are challenged to discover what their gifts were and the opportunities that were offered to them, they wanted to be stewards of those gifts and opportunities. They wanted to be responsible. If you have not been a steward of your gifts, this is the time to make a change in your life. If you are a good steward of your gifts, then you will be an effective person. The responsible steward is really the most blessed, not necessarily the most talented. In the next day or two take an assignment given you from either your parents or a teacher and do it to the max. This will demonstrate that you are a steward of your ability to follow through. Accomplish this and you will experience the blessing. The stewards receives in their lives the blessings the Lord proclaims come to that good steward. The Lord said "Come, you who are blessed of My Father, inherit the kingdom prepared for you from the foundation of the world (Matthew 25: 34 (NAB)."

#34: <u>Se</u> = Selenium = <u>Se</u>rvant

## THE CALL

Teens desire to be leaders among their peers and in their schools. But to be a true leader, one must be a servant. This is the model we are given in the Bible. If you want to be a godly person, you are called to serve others. Selenium is known to have incredible attributes such as taking light and converting it into electricity, energy. An element using what it is, is being a servant with its ability to give energy to something other than itself. A Christian teen needs to make one's presence known by one's effect on others, that is, being a servant.

THE WORD OF GOD SAYS...

Matthew 20:32 (RSV)
[32] And Jesus stopped and called them, saying, "What do you want me to do for you?"

Mark 10:43–44 (RSV)
[43] But it shall not be so among you; but whoever would be great among you must be your servant, [44] and whoever would be first among you must be slave of all.

Luke 1:38 (RSV)
[38] And Mary said, "Behold, I am the handmaid of the Lord; let it be to me according to your word." And the angel departed from her.

Psalm 35:27 (RSV)
[27] Let those who desire my vindication shout for joy and be glad, and say evermore, "Great is the LORD, who delights in the welfare of his servant!"

Romans 1:1 (RSV)
[1] Paul, a servant of Jesus Christ, called to be an apostle, set apart for the gospel of God

2 Timothy 2:24 (RSV)
[24] And the Lord's servant must not be quarrelsome but kindly to every one, an apt teacher, forebearing,

## THE CHALLENGE

It is a difficult call to be a servant. If you want to be most like Christ you need to follow the one person who was most like Christ on earth, the exemplar model of all Christians, the Blessed Mother. She made it clear in accepting her call to be the Mother of God that the will of God should be done, not hers. That is how it must be with you. If the Lord was servant to His apostles (washing their feet) then the example is clear. The promise of the Lord is, that if you give up your lives (Mark 10:43-44) in service, then you find it. What a tremendous gift you receive from God's mighty grace for your being a servant. You become a leader. Think of a way that you can this week, do something to demonstrate that you are a servant of the Lord to your parents, a teacher, your pastor, your peers. St. Paul (2 Timothy 2:24) tells you what you need to do to be a good servant, namely, be kind, a good teacher and forebearing ( meaning being patient). Therefore, be a good servant.

#52: **Te** = Tellurium = **Te**mperance

## THE CALL

Temperance is one of the cardinal virtues. Temperance is usually thought of as having to do with avoiding the excess drinking of alcohol. But it also applies to one's ability to develop a habit of "moderation in the indulgence of appetites and passions" as Webster's Dictionary defines it. Tellurium has as one of its uses the tinting of glass. Does your car have tinted windows? It moderates the amount of light that can get through. As a cardinal virtue temperance is defined in the Catechism of the Catholic Church as "the moral virtue that moderates the attraction of pleasures and provides balance in the use of created goods." (CCC #1809) Life needs something to control evil, lack of temperance or moderation. The virtue of temperance is that moderator for life. It is the virtue that means to also be sober in life, and not just by staying away from alcohol.

## THE WORD OF GOD SAYS...

Titus 2:11-12 (RSV)
[11] For the grace of God has appeared for the salvation of all men, [12] training us to renounce irreligion and worldly passions, and to live sober, upright, and godly lives in this world.

Sirach 18: 30 (RSV)
[30] Do not follow your base desires, but restrain your appetites.

1 Thessalonians 5:6 (RSV)
[6] So then let us not sleep, as others do, but let us keep awake and be sober.

1 Peter 5:8 (RSV)
[8] Be sober, be watchful. Your adversary the devil prowls around like a roaring lion, seeking some one to devour.

1 Thessalonians 5:8 (RSV)
[8] But, since we belong to the day, let us be sober, and put on the breastplate of faith and love, and for a helmet the hope of salvation.

1 Peter 5:8 (RSV)
[8] Be sober, be watchful. Your adversary the devil prowls around like a roaring lion, seeking some one to devour.

## THE CHALLENGE

It is easy to see that this cardinal virtue (one of four virtues so named) is a difficult one for the modern millennial teen to strive to live. This virtue really calls for a great deal of self-control. There is so much excess to distract and tempt the teen today. Therefore, your efforts to keep this virtue need to be stepped up to the max. It is not easy for you to open a magazine, the newspaper, or most programs on television and not see passions of people's lives displayed without any control. You have to develop that discipline of character to have the moderation that the bible speaks of. Especially is this true with regard to sex and alcohol. Too many teens think of these two areas as modes of recreation. They are not. You must practice temperance with regard to them. Discipline yourself to do this. If you see yourself giving in to these passions and appetites then you need to do something to change your attention. Perhaps you can do some fasting to train you not to focus on this lack of virtue. If you find yourself controlled by sexual passion, for example, why not give up that can of soda you have at lunch every day. Or even better, give it up for the whole day. Watch how the discipline of your body can lead you to more control, and then you will have temperance. You will need to have your eyes tinted to protect you from the sinfulness of sexual fantasies. Sound impossible? It is not, you can do it. Remember, it is a decision you can make.

#84: **Po** = Polonium = **Po**ndering

## THE CALL

Polonium is a radioactive element that occurs naturally in very low concentrations in the earth's crust. Polonium can be taken into the body by eating food, drinking water, or breathing air. Studies of smokers have shown that inhaled polonium can be highly localized in the lungs, with about twice as much polonium found in the ribs of smokers compared to nonsmokers. *(Argonne National Laboratory, EVS).* Polonium is not very stable, and it is said that a small sample will evaporate in a few days. It does not stay around long, it is as though it is not there for one to ponder (that is to consider or to take a second look at it). Life sometimes just evaporates from you also if you do not take the time to ponder what God is doing in your life. Time is a great way to see God's work, but it does take time.

THE WORD OF GOD SAYS...

Luke 2: 19 (NIV)
[19] But Mary treasured up all these things and pondered them in her heart.

Proverbs 4:26 (KJV)
[26] Ponder the path of thy feet, and let all thy ways be established.

Isaiah 43:18 (NAS)
[18] Do not call to mind the former things, or ponder things of the past.

THE CHALLENGE

Teens live in a busy world. "Do it quickly" seems to be what drives you most. Think of how much you like fast foods, get it now, no waiting. Maybe this also affects how you relate to the Lord. Do you rush through prayer or reading the Bible? If you are always in a hurry and rushing, you will miss some great things the Lord has for you. Rushing instead of pondering things keeps you from appreciating many things, even God. Rushing reminds me a lot like polonium, which is radioactive and disintegrates rather rapidly. You chemistry students know about the half-life of radioactive elements. I love the term half-life, which is not full-life. That is what happens if you rush and do not ponder a relationship with the Lord.

If you have not had the experience of pondering, then you are just living a life of ease and not a life of meaning. Without taking time to ponder decisions, you are simply taking the easy way out. Look for a time of struggle ahead. It is very much like an athlete who does not ponder his next move on the court. He just takes a shot, and it goes nowhere. He was not pondering, but just acting. Take the time to ponder. It is hard work, but it does produce good results.

Try something new. Think of pondering (slowing down, thinking) when you pray and when you read the Bible. Take a passage of the Bible. Read it. Re-read it, but this time slowly, ask what is the meaning for you. That is what pondering is all about. Also, this week ask yourself have you taken time for your family. Ponder that idea and ask if your time with your parents is what God is asking of you. Ponder what they ask you to do or what they have suggested for you. Unless you get into the habit of pondering, not only God's words in the Bible , but also in your life, you will miss many exciting possibilities in your life.

# 11

## THE JOURNEY WITH GROUP 17 THE HALOGENS AND THE RELATED VIRTUES TO THE SYMBOLS OF THIS GROUP

The members of this family of group 17 known as the Halogens has some very familiar elements that you know and use. The virtues related to the symbols of this group are mighty testimonials to solid virtuous living.

HALOGENS GROUP 17

CHEMICAL ELEMENT:          SPIRITUAL ELEMENT OF
                          VIRTUE:

Number: Name: Symbol

| | | | |
|---|---|---|
| 9 Fluorine | F | **F**aithfulness |
| 17 Chlorine | Cl | **C**onsistent **l**oyalty |
| 35 Bromine | Br | **Br**otherhood |
| 53 Iodine | I | **I**ntegrity |
| 85 Astatine | At | **At**onement |

#9: **F** = Fluorine = **F**aithfulness

## THE CALL

Faithfulness to God and His Church is an incredible source of protection for you and your life. Fluorine, in the natural world, is important for our lives. You probably know it best because it is added to drinking water and toothpastes to help provide strong teeth. I grew up in Denver, Colorado, where our water was naturally rich in Fluorine and as a result we have strong teeth and few cavities. Would you also love that? Nature provides a great protection for us. God, through our faithfulness to Him also provides a great protection to us.

## THE WORD OF GOD SAYS...

Psalm 25:10 (RSV)
[10] All the paths of the LORD are steadfast love and faithfulness, for those who keep his covenant and his testimonies.

Psalm 26:3 (RSV)
[3] For thy steadfast love is before my eyes, and I walk in faithfulness to thee.

Psalm 33:4 (RSV)
[4] For the word of the LORD is upright; and all his work is done in faithfulness.

Psalm 89:1 (RSV)
[1] I will sing of thy steadfast love, O LORD, for ever; with my mouth I will proclaim thy faithfulness to all generations.

Hebrews 13:5 (RSV)
⁵ Keep your life free from love of money, and be content with what you have; for he has said, "I will never fail you nor forsake you."

Psalm 91:4 (RSV)
⁴ he will cover you with his pinions, and under his wings you will find refuge; his faithfulness is a shield and buckler.

THE CHALLENGE

You read it God will never fail you, never forsake you. This is God's promise. What a sign of encouragement especially for young people. There is such a lack of faithfulness among many of your peers and it becomes almost an infection. Your challenge is not to give in to unfaithfulness. See what you can do to express your faithfulness to God by giving witness to how you believe in the truths of our Church. Maybe you could even invite a good friend to be faithful in attending Mass with you each week.

#17: **Cl** = Chlorine = **C**onsistent **l**oyalty

THE CALL

Chlorine is well known in our world. All of you have had an experience of it. It is used extensively to purify and clarify water, and we say it is chlorinated. You may even have had the unfortunate experience of smelling it in the water from your tap. It has a bleach smell like mother knows from using bleach doing laundry. Bleach has chlorine in it. The person who follows Christ wants to be one who has CONSISTENT LOYALTY.

This is a call to be sure that we are purified as His followers. If you are purified then you are a person who has consistent loyalty to Jesus. Remember it must be consistent and not just loyalty.

THE WORD OF GOD SAYS...

Psalm 101:1 (RSV)
[1] I will sing of loyalty and of justice; to thee, O LORD, I will sing.

Proverbs 16:6 (RSV)
[6] By loyalty and faithfulness iniquity is atoned for,
and by the fear of the LORD a man avoids evil.

Hebrews 13:8–9 (RSV)
[8] Jesus Christ is the same yesterday and today and for ever. [9] Do not be led away by diverse and strange teachings; for it is well that the heart be strengthened by grace, not by foods, which have not benefited their adherents

Malachi 3:6–7 (RSV)
[6] For I the LORD do not change; therefore you, O sons of Jacob, are not consumed. [7] From the days of your fathers you have turned aside from my statutes and have not kept them. Return to me, and I will return to you, says the LORD of hosts. But you say, 'How shall we return?'

THE CHALLENGE

It is not enough to be consistent but that your consistency must be loyal.

Consistency and Loyalty to God is necessary if you are to be a person of integrity before the Lord. You cannot have a good relationship if it is not consistent and loyal. The Lord is ever consistent, He is always there for you, always ready to respond to your needs. Solid as the famous rock of Gibraltar is the Lord. Then add to that His loyalty to you. He never abandons you. Now it is time for you to examine some of your relationships with your parents, family and your friends. Are they consistent and loyal? If you have some doubts about it, it may be helpful to examine your relationship with the Lord first. If that is not consistent and loyal, then you cannot expect to have those virtues with your family and friends. Let the Lord be your model for all relationships. The Psalms tell us that "for the Lord protects those who are loyal to Him." ( Psalm 31:23)

#35: **Br** = Bromine = **Br**otherhood

THE CALL

If you are a male teen and have been involved in any kind of team activity you know in some small way what the meaning of brotherhood is all about. It is an incredible experience and gift that God gives. Once you have experienced it you will find it a treasure for the rest of your life. Bromine is important as a part of many medicines and water purification processes. For bromine to work it must be added to other substances. Therefore, its function in the natural world, is something added to other things to make them useful. Just as brotherhood is something added to a person's life to make it more useful and meaningful. The gift of brotherhood is well established as a spiritual gift. Take a read at what God's word has to say about it.

## THE WORD OF GOD SAYS...

**1 Peter 2:17 (RSV)**
[17] Honor all men. Love the brotherhood. Fear God. Honor the emperor.

**4 Maccabees 9:23 (RSV)**
[23] "Imitate me, brothers," he said. "Do not leave your post in my struggle or renounce our courageous brotherhood."

**1 Peter 5:8–9 (RSV)**
[8] Be sober, be watchful. Your adversary the devil prowls around like a roaring lion, seeking some one to devour. [9] Resist him, firm in your faith, knowing that the same experience of suffering is required of your brotherhood throughout the world.

**1 Peter 2:16–17 (RSV)**
[16] Live as free men, yet without using your freedom as a pretext for evil; but live as servants of God. [17] Honor all men. Love the brotherhood. Fear God. Honor the emperor.

## THE CHALLENGE

"Love the brotherhood " (I Peter 2:17) What could say it clearer. But to love the brotherhood, one has to live the brotherhood. Seek to have a brotherhood with other good Christian teens. Seek them out in your school or in your parish youth program. There is nothing so special as being a part of the brotherhood. It is the modern expression of knighthood. This was a noble calling in the days of knighthood. It was a respected position a young man sought and when granted the title of knight, and the brotherhood it formed, was lived with respect and honor.

Would that you could have that today among young teens. You really need to seek how this could happen. Start talking to other teens you know to be godly and good men of faith, and see what you can do to start a brotherhood. It will be a great way to avoid falling into the hands of the devil and his evil ways or the ways the world would have you fall into. It will preserve you, because of faithfulness to the brotherhood and to the church. It will also preserve you from falling into bad habits of behavior such as pornography and sex outside of marriage. Go for it. God will bless it.

#53: **I** = Iodine = **I**ntegrity

## THE CALL

Life requires that we have ways to be purified and cleansed. Iodine, mixed in an alcohol solution, is used as a disinfectant to cleanse wounds. Life has wounds and many of these wounds are in a person's character and often due to a lack of INTEGRITY. That lack can be corrected by having a right relationship with God. To do this one has to live as God asks you to live. Having a relationship with God and living as He asks are basic elements of INTEGRITY. What clearly activates INTEGRITY is a purified life, cleansed of the sins in our world and centered in the Lord.

## THE WORD OF GOD SAYS...

2 Timothy 2:21 (RSV)
[21] If any one purifies himself from what is ignoble, then he will be a vessel for noble use, consecrated and useful to the master of the house, ready for any good work.

Psalm 7:8 (RSV)
[8] The Lord judges the peoples; judge me, O Lord, according to my righteousness and according to the integrity that is in me.

Proverbs 28:6 (RSV)
[6] Better is a poor man who walks in his integrity than a rich man who is perverse in his ways.

1 Peter 2:12 (RSV)
[12] Maintain good conduct among the Gentiles, so that in case they speak against you as wrongdoers, they may see your good deeds and glorify God on the day of visitation.

Titus 2:7–8 (RSV)
[7] Show yourself in all respects a model of good deeds, and in your teaching show integrity, gravity, [8] and sound speech that cannot be censured, so that an opponent may be put to shame, having nothing evil to say of us.

## THE CHALLENGE

God's call to be a young person who lives in goodness is no easy task. But God does call you to this goal. To be that person of goodness means that you must be a person of INTEGRITY. You need to show your INTEGRITY, in our world that is not very much in tune with our Christian faith. It is a world that is filled with many temptations and evils that will attack you if you want to live the INTEGRITY that God is calling you to live. Be on your guard watching at every moment how the evils around you can really destroy you as a person. Seek the support and help of God (we call it grace) in being one who goes to reconciliation on a regular basis. This is a great way to be accountable to God. This will help you maintain INTEGRITY in every aspect of being a teen of INTEGRITY. Try doing two things to help you develop integrity. First, set boundaries for your behavior. Stay in bounds and you can make a winning score as in football. Second, do not rationalize. That means you cannot say something like, "everyone is doing it." That will not work for you. Do these two things this week and see how you are growing in integrity.

#85: **At** = Astatine = **At**onement

THE CALL

Nature sometimes gives us things that are not long for this world. Astatine is one of those elements. It is said that it is highly radioactive and none of it exists except in laboratories. It is another of those elements that has a very short half-life therefore, not much is known about it. It is kind of a forgotten element.

To forget is kind of what happened when Jesus made Atonement for us. He stepped up and did the atonement (reconciliation) for our sins with God. Because He did this through His sacrificial death, our sins were forgotten, atoned, cleansed. Therefore, in the language of God we can look at the idea of atonement as meaning at-one-ment. Simply stated it really means getting us back together and at peace with God. What Jesus did by His death was to bring us back to God taking away the bad things we do by our sins.

THE WORD OF GOD SAYS...

While the word atonement does not actually occur in our New Testament Bible translations today, the meaning of it is clearly seen in several of the following passages of God's word.

Leviticus 23:26–29 (RSV)
[26] And the LORD said to Moses, [27] "On the tenth day of this seventh month is the day of atonement; it shall be for you a time of holy convocation, and you shall afflict yourselves and present an offering by fire to the LORD. [28] And you shall do no work on this same day; for it is a day of atonement, to make atonement for you before the LORD your God. [29] For whoever is not afflicted on this same day shall be cut off from his people.

1 Corinthians 15:3–5 (RSV)
[3] For I delivered to you as of first importance what I also received, that Christ died for our sins in accordance with the scriptures, [4] that he was buried, that he was raised on the third day in accordance with the scriptures, [5] and that he appeared to Cephas, then to the twelve.

Matthew 1: 21 (RSV)
[21] she will bear a son, and you shall call his name Jesus, for he will save his people from their sins.

John 10:14–15 (RSV)
[14] I am the good shepherd; I know my own and my own know me, [15] as the Father knows me and I know the Father; and I lay down my life for the sheep.

Romans 3:21–26 (RSV)
[21] But now the righteousness of God has been manifested apart from law, although the law and the prophets bear witness to it, [22] the righteousness of God through faith in Jesus Christ for all who believe. For there is no distinction; [23] since all have sinned and fall short of the glory of God, [24] they are justified by his grace as a gift, through the redemption which is in Christ Jesus,

[25] whom God put forward as an expiation by his blood, to be received by faith. This was to show God's righteousness, because in his divine forbearance he had passed over former sins; [26] it was to prove at the present time that he himself is righteous and that he justifies him who has faith in Jesus.

## THE CHALLENGE

The idea of atonement should be a twofold celebration. Re-read the above scriptures and see how God in the Old Testament required a time of atonement from the people so that they could make a reconciliation with God. Then you have a reason to celebrate the understanding of atonement, or reconciliation, in the New Testament. The gift to celebrate is what Jesus did for us. It was His Atonement that set us free. Now it is your time to do something positive to say thanks to the Lord for that gift. Think of what you can do for someone this week who is in need of your help. It might be that you are very good at math. Look for a classmate who is having problems with math and offer to tutor them. You might be very good at singing therefore offer to help with the music program at your parish youth program. Are you good at some sport? A great gift would be to offer your time to help at an elementary school sports program to help the young children learn whatever your sport of choice may be. These are ways you can imitate a kind of atonement that people of the Old Testament did. Do it and you will find that you have great comfort in doing for others.

# 12

## THE JOURNEY ENDS WITH GROUP 18 THE NOBLE GASES AND THEIR RELATED VIRTUES

The members of this family group 18 are known as the Noble Gases also have the name of Inert Gases. These are generally well known elements. Our virtues related to their symbols are not as well known, but nonetheless important virtues for a heroic virtuous life.

NOBLE (INERT) GASES GROUP 18

| CHEMICAL ELEMENT: | SPIRITUAL ELEMENT OF VIRTUE: |
|---|---|
| Number: Name: Symbol | |

| | | |
|---|---|---|
| 2 Helium | He | **He**aven |
| 10 Neon | Ne | **Ne**w Creation |
| 18 Argon | Ar | **Ar**dor |
| 36 Krypton | Kr | **K**inetic **r**everence |
| 54 Xenon | Xe | **Xe**nophilia |
| 86 Radon | Rn | **R**ighteous **n**eighbor |

#2: **He** = Helium = **He**aven

THE CALL

We are made for Heaven. Interesting it comes after a life of holiness that we reach heaven. As we know, this is what we were created for and that is our goal of life. Helium comes after hydrogen. It is the first of the noble gases. How noble is it for us to want to get to heaven. It is a complete place, similar to the nobleness of helium, heaven does not have to react with anything else to provide completeness for us.

THE WORD OF GOD SAYS...

Psalm 69:34 (RSV)
[34] Let heaven and earth praise him, the seas and everything that moves therein.

Psalm 57:3 (RSV)
[3] He will send from heaven and save me, he will put to shame those who trample upon me. [Selah] God will send forth his steadfast love and his faithfulness!

Psalm 73:25 (RSV)
[25] Whom have I in heaven but thee? And there is nothing upon earth that I desire besides thee.

Ecclesiastes 3:1 (RSV)
[1] For everything there is a season, and a time for every matter under heaven:

Matthew 5:12 (RSV)
[12] Rejoice and be glad, for your reward is great in heaven, for so men persecuted the prophets who were before you.

John 6:50 (RSV)
[50] This is the bread which comes down from heaven, that a man may eat of it and not die.

John 3:27 (RSV)
[27] John answered, "No one can receive anything except what is given him from heaven."

Romans 1:18 (RSV)
[18] For the wrath of God is revealed from heaven against all ungodliness and wickedness of men who by their wickedness suppress the truth.

## THE CHALLENGE

God's word calls you to search and seek for the heavenly kingdom. How refreshing this is from the search and seeking for worthless worldly values. You do not have to search for sex, pornography, and lustful thoughts. They will not get you to heaven. Be an advocate that promotes among your peers the virtues of a holy young man or young woman. You can be a leader among your peers and watch how they follow your strength of character. Recall that as you seek holiness you are also promised a great reward, which is heaven. All that you have and are is "given us from heaven." Heaven is our home, seek it always and walk in the ways of your life that will get you there. It is the way of no fear and no doubts. How great is that? Do something incredible this week that will help you along that way to heaven. It might be something as giving some of your time one day in the week to go to daily Mass. Watch how differently you act throughout the day.

#10: **Ne** = Neon = **Ne**w Creation

## THE CALL

Neon is an interesting element. We know it most from its common uses in our world today. You probably think of advertising signs, when you hear neon. Yes, "neon lights." You might also know that it is used in making TV tubes and gas lasers. The gas lasers are interesting, since they can be used to indicate a clear direction and a powerful light source. With that in mind, the Lord calls you to be a new creation. He wants you to be His advertising sign to your peers and he wants you to be a penetrating light in the world of millennia teens.

## THE WORD OF GOD SAYS...

2 Corinthians 5:17 (RSV)
[17] Therefore, if any one is in Christ, he is a new creation; the old has passed away, behold, the new has come.

Galatians 6:15 (RSV)
[15] For neither circumcision counts for anything, nor uncircumcision, but a new creation.

Romans 7:6 (RSV)
[6] But now we are discharged from the law, dead to that which held us captive, so that we serve not under the old written code but in the new life of the Spirit.

## THE CHALLENGE

It is not easy to be that new creation in today's world, but as the Lord told us, nothing is impossible with Him. Seek the Lord each day in your life and know that you will be that powerful "sign" and "beam". You will be a magnificent manifestation of His power in you through His grace that will allow you to speak forth for the faith with the strength and directness of a spiritual laser beam. It is not impossible for teens to do this. You need to act with confidence and courage of your faith to do it. Sometime this week seek out teens who look confused and going in the wrong direction. Give them a sense of your truthful direction as you follow the Lord and ask them to join you in being a new "advertising sign" for Jesus. Then there will be two strong lights or beams of truth to enlighten the direction of more teens.

#18: **Ar** = Argon = **Ar**dor

## THE CALL

Ardor and argon sound alike and there is some relational ideas about both of them that are alike. Argon is important in nature for the metal industry. Ask your dad or a friend if he knows what arc welding is all about. That is what argon ( an inert gas) is used for. It is also used for cutting of metals and in electric light bulbs, like the fluorescent tubes in your classroom at school. Ardor, in the spiritual side of your life is a sense of fervor that you have for the gift of faith that has been given you. Ardor or enthusiasm is another way of saying what passion do you have for your faith.

## THE WORD OF GOD SAYS...

Acts 18:25 (RSV)
[25] He had been instructed in the way of the Lord; and being fervent in spirit, he spoke and taught accurately the things concerning Jesus, though he knew only the baptism of John.

Romans 12:11(NIV)
[11] Never be lacking in zeal, but keep your spiritual fervor, serving the Lord.

Isaiah 42:13 (NAB)
[13] The LORD goes forth like a hero, like a warrior he stirs up his ardor; He shouts out his battle cry, against his enemies he shows his might.

I Macabees 6: 47 (NAB)
[47] When the Jews saw the strength of the royal army and the ardor of its forces, they retreated from them.

## THE CHALLENGE

There is nothing more exciting than seeing the ardor of teens excited about their faith. It is a truism to say that when teens express their fervor for faith it has an infective result on other teens. Maybe you need to be like St. Ignatius of Loyola, who, in his writings, had such ardor for the kingdom of God, that they transformed the reader. That is what it is for the teen as well. Think of it for a moment, for example, what most excites you? Is it your love for your parents? Is it your ardor for the sport of your choice, the music style that you like, or a subject in school. If you have an ardor for it, you will soar to success with it. Now translate some of that ardor, that excitement, for the Lord who by His death on the cross has given you the incredible gift of faith. Try one day this week to express your excitement about your faith to another teen, or even an adult. Watch what that ardor (excitement) will do for them.

#36: **Kr** = Krypton = **K**inetic **r**everence

THE CALL

You have all heard of krypton. No doubt it was in connection with the Superman movies. It of course was used as a name of the planet in the world of make believe. In nature krypton is another of the group called noble gases. Its use is like argon, as an agent to help flourescent lights do what they are supposed to do. But think of it, they release energy (release of energy is called kinetic). That is why you should release energy, and this is called kinetic reverence for the Lord's goodness to you. Don't live your life just with potential reverence (like potential energy which is energy not at work). If you have received any gift there should be a sense of this kinetic reverence for it.

THE WORD OF GOD SAYS...

1 Peter 3:14–15 (RSV)
[14] But even if you do suffer for righteousness' sake, you will be blessed. Have no fear of them, nor be troubled, [15] but in your hearts reverence Christ as Lord. Always be prepared to make a defense to any one who calls you to account for the hope that is in you, yet do it with gentleness and reverence;

Psalm 2:11 (NASB)
<sup>11</sup> Worship the LORD with reverence And rejoice with trembling.

Hebrews 12:28 (NASB)
<sup>28</sup> Therefore, since we receive a kingdom which cannot be shaken, let us show gratitude, by which we may offer to God an acceptable service with reverence and awe.

Ephesians 5:21 (RSV)
<sup>21</sup> Be subject to one another out of reverence for Christ.

1 Peter 3:15 (RSV)
<sup>15</sup> but in your hearts reverence Christ as Lord. Always be prepared to make a defense to any one who calls you to account for the hope that is in you, yet do it with gentleness and reverence.

4 Maccabees 17:15 (RSV)
<sup>15</sup> Reverence for God was victor and gave the crown to its own athletes.

Psalm 5:8 (NAB)
<sup>8</sup> But I can enter your house because of your great love.
I can worship in your holy temple because of my reverence for you, LORD.

Ephesians 5:21 (NIV)
<sup>21</sup> Submit to one another out of reverence for Christ.

Hebrews 5:7 (NAB)
<sup>7</sup> In the days when he (Melchizedek) was in the flesh, he offered prayers and supplications with loud cries and tears to the one

who was able to save him from death, and he was heard because of his reverence.

## THE CHALLENGE

It is really important to have this kinetic reverence because this is what will allow the Lord to hear you (Hebrews 5:7). If you have this reverence for the Lord it is really alive with energy (kinetic) then you will be showing that reverence not merely out of routine observance. Instead it will be shown because you have that alive energy to want to reverence God in all things. This will exhibit itself in many ways. Of course, the first way is always reverence for the name of God. Another way is reverence for your parents, thanking God for the gift of life that they have given you. You can also have this alive energy of reverence for all things. Therefore, it would be wrong for someone to be a tagger, marking up other people's things or property. You would not want someone to mark up your things. Therefore, why is this such a problem for many young people? Is it that they do not know the commandments of God. Make it your project this coming week to try to talk to someone you might know who does not reverence other people or property. This is what God expects from you.

#54: **Xe** = Xenon = **Xe**nophilia

## THE CALL

Xenophilia, this is a strange word. Check it out in the dictionary and we find it really is a neat word. Xenon is a Greek word that means "stranger" and philia comes from a Greek word that means "love." Therefore, it means to love the stranger. When

Xenon was discovered they could not find enough of the substance. It was a "stranger" in the lab, hence the name Xenon. This is an amazing connection to our faith as we are taught to be kind to all. We need to love the stranger as well as the friend. Jesus was always friendly and loving to all He met even strangers. We need to learn to be welcoming of those who are strangers in our midst.

THE WORD OF GOD SAYS...

Math 25: 35 (RSV)
[35] for I was hungry an you gave me food, I was thirsty and you gave me drink, I was a stranger and you welcomed me.

Psalm 146: 9 (NAB)
[9] The Lord protects the stranger, sustains the orphan and the widow, but thwarts the way of the wicked.

Proverbs 27:13 (NAB)
[13] Take his garment who becomes surety for another, and for the sake of a stranger, yield it up!

Matthew 25:43 (RSV)
[43] I was a stranger and you did not welcome me, naked and you did not clothe me, sick and in prison and you did not visit me.'

Leviticus 19:34 (RSV)
[34] The stranger who sojourns with you shall be to you as the native among you, and you shall love him as yourself; for you were strangers in the land of Egypt: I am the LORD your God.

## THE CHALLENGE

It is difficult to be a stranger in a strange land as we read in the Bible. You may have had that occur to you. Were you ever a transfer student in high school? You will know what it meant to be a stranger. You would have hoped that someone would have desired to meet you (Xenophilia). If that was your feeling then the challenge is to extend a welcome to strangers in your parish youth group or your school. Go up to them and introduce yourself and welcome them to the parish community or the school community. When you start to see Christ in the stranger you start to be more like Him. One who follows Jesus is a stranger and pilgrim in this world--a world which is passing away from its focus on the Lord. Today, teens who follow the Lord and are proud to be Catholic are much like St. Francis Xavier when he came as a stranger to India to bring the message of our Church to the people of that land. Imitate St. Francis and bring the message of our faith to others who do not know the Lord in your school.

#86: **Rn** = Radon = **R**ighteous **n**eighbor

## THE CALL

Radon is the last of the group called a noble gases. Chemically it is a radioactive, colorless, odorless, tasteless noble gas. Radon is found in nature as a decay product of radium. Since it is radioactive it is considered a health hazard. Because it is radioactive and has a very short half-life, about four days, meaning half of it would be gone is four days. What is interesting is that it is a noble gas. This gives us the reason to consider a spiritual metaphor for Radon (Rn) that being a righteous neighbor.

That would be a noble task. Unlike radon, which has a short existence, a righteous neighbor can have lifelong effects. Being a righteous neighbor is something you are called to be as followers of the Lord.

THE WORD OF GOD SAYS...

Being righteous is one of the most often found concepts in the scriptures. Let us look at a few.

Proverbs 12:26-28 (RSV)
[26] A righteous man turns away from evil, but the way of the wicked leads them astray. [27] A slothful man will not catch his prey, but the diligent man will get precious wealth. [28] In the path of righteousness is life, but the way of error leads to death.

Proverbs 10:6–7 (RSV)
[6] Blessings are on the head of the righteous, but the mouth of the wicked conceals violence. [7] The memory of the righteous is a blessing, but the name of the wicked will rot.

Sirach 35:7 (RSV)
[7] The sacrifice of a righteous man is acceptable, and the memory of it will not be forgotten.

Galatians 3:11 (RSV)
[11] Now it is evident that no man is justified before God by the law; for "He who through faith is righteous shall live";

Romans 1:17 (RSV)
[17] For in it the righteousness of God is revealed through faith

for faith; as it is written, "He who through faith is righteous shall live."

Psalm 64:10 (RSV)
[10] Let the righteous rejoice in the LORD, and take refuge in him! Let all the upright in heart glory!

Psalm 92:12 (RSV)
[12] The righteous flourish like the palm tree, and grow like a cedar in Lebanon.

## THE CHALLENGE

You may ask why do I want to be a righteous neighbor? God has a great answer: "so that you can get to heaven." What a gift for being righteous! The expectation of being a righteous neighbor is very simple. Do what is right, that is it. Remember Jesus removed your sins by His death on the cross. He was a righteous neighbor. Remember the good thief was forgiven by the Lord and told he would be with the Lord in heaven. No less for you. If you are doing what is right, you are being a righteous person.

Remember if you are doing what is right and being a righteous person you will get to heaven. Recall the Bible statements above and see the blessings promised, it is heaven. Being a righteous neighbor, your peers may say some strange and negative things about you. Always remember that if you are doing what is right, then those negative things just mean that the speakers are not righteous before God, and they may even be vindictive. If that happens to you the best way to handle them is to rely on God and always react with a positive response. That is the right thing, and you remain a righteous neighbor. This week at school, try to be a great example of being a righteous neighbor (classmate). Say something positive about your neighbor. See what happens. In addition, you might try to do a good deed for an elderly neighbor where you live. Just go over and do something nice for them. Take out the trash, mow the lawn, take them shopping. Good things happen to the righteous neighbor. God promises us in His words of the Bible, and He always delivers.

# APPENDIX ONE
# PERIODIC CHART OF VIRTUES
# COMPARISON WITH ELEMENTS

CHEMICAL ELEMENT:    SPIRITUAL ELEMENT OF
VIRTUE:

Number: Name: Symbol

ALKALI METALS GROUP 1

| | | |
|---|---|---|
| 1 Hydrogen | H | **H**oliness |
| 3 Lithium | Li | **Li**ght |
| 11 Sodium | Na | **Na**vigate God |
| 19 Potassium | K | **K**indness |
| 37 Rubidium | Rb | **R**ighteous **b**eing |
| 55 Cesium | Cs | **C**hristian **s**trength |
| 87 Francium | Fr | **Fr**iendship |

## ALKALINE EARTH METALS Group 2

| | | |
|---|---|---|
| 4 Beryllium | Be | **Be**lief |
| 12 Magnesium | Mg | **M**ountain of **G**od |
| 20 Calcium | Ca | **Ca**ring |
| 38 Strontium | Sr | **S**piritual **r**edemption |
| 56 Barium | Ba | **Ba**lance |
| 88 Radium | Ra | **Ra**diate |

## GROUP 3 TO 7 TRANSITION METALS (PART ONE)

## GROUP 3:

| | | |
|---|---|---|
| 21 Scandium | Sc | **Sc**holars for the Lord |
| 39 Yttrium | Y | **Y**ield to the Lord |

## GROUP 4:

| | | |
|---|---|---|
| 22 Titanium | Ti | **Ti**thing |
| 40 Zirconium | Zr | **Z**eal **r**eborn |
| 72 Hafnium | Hf | **H**oly **F**amily |

## LANTHANIDES GROUP 4f

| | | |
|---|---|---|
| 57 Lanthanum | La | **La**ughter |
| 58 Cerium | Ce | **Ce**lebrate |
| 59 Praseodymium | Pr | **Pr**udence |
| 60 Neodymium | Nd | **N**on-**d**estructive |
| 61 Promethium | Pm | **P**ro-**m**agnanimous |
| 62 Samarium | Sm | **Sm**ile |

## GROUP 5:

| 23 Vanadium | V | **V**isionary |
|---|---|---|
| 41 Niobium | Nb | **N**ot **b**oasting |
| 73 Tantalum | Ta | **Ta**bernacle Time |

## ACTINIDES GROUP 5f

| 89 Actinium | Ac | **Ac**countable |
|---|---|---|
| 90 Thorium | Th | **Th**ankfulness |
| 91 Protactinium | Pa | **Pa**radise |
| 92 Uranium | U | **U**nity |

## GROUP 6:

| 24 Chromium | Cr | **Cr**edibility |
|---|---|---|
| 42 Molybdenum | Mo | **Mo**rality |
| 74 Tungsten | W | **W**isdom |

## GROUP 7:

| 25 Manganese | Mn | **M**oral **n**orms |
|---|---|---|
| 43 Technetium | Tc | **T**rue **c**ontrition |
| 75 Rhenium | Re | **Re**verence |

## GROUP 8 TO 12 TRANSITION METALS (PART TWO)

## GROUP 8:

| 26 Iron | Fe | **Fe**llowship |
|---|---|---|
| 44 Ruthenium | Ru | **Ru**thlike |
| 76 Osmium | Os | **Os**tracize |

## GROUP 9:

| 27 Cobalt | Co | **Co**mpassion |
| 45 Rhodium | Rh | **R**adical **h**umility |
| 77 Iridium | Ir | **Ir**reproachable |

## GROUP 10:

| 28 Nickel | Ni | **Ni**ce |
| 46 Palladium | Pd | **Pd**-in-full |
| 78 Platinum | Pt | **P**rayer **T**ime |

## GROUP 11:

| 29 Copper | Cu | **Cu**ltivate the faith |
| 47 Silver | Ag | **Ag**reeable |
| 79 Gold | Au | **Au**thentic |

## GROUP 12:

| 30 Zinc | Zn | **Z**ealous **n**ature |
| 48 Cadmium | Cd | **C**hrist **d**oer |
| 80 Mercury | Hg | **H**oly **g**uidelines |

## GROUP 13: BORON FAMILY

| 5 Boron | B | **B**lessings |
| 13 Aluminum | Al | **Al**mighty God |
| 31 Gallium | Ga | **Ga**llant |
| 49 Indium | In | **In**dwelling of the Holy Spirit |
| 81 Thallium | Tl | **T**enacious **l**iving |

## GROUP 14: CARBON FAMILY

| | | |
|---|---|---|
| 6 Carbon | C | **C**atholic |
| 14 Silicon | Si | **Si**lence |
| 32 Germanium | Ge | **Ge**nerosity |
| 50 Tin | Sn | **S**teadfast **n**ature |
| 82 Lead | Pb | **P**erfect **b**ook |

## GROUP 15: NITROGEN FAMILY

| | | |
|---|---|---|
| 7 Nitrogen | N | **N**ear us |
| 15 Phosphorous | P | **P**rayerful |
| 33 Arsenic | As | **A**ffirming **s**pirit |
| 51 Antimony | Sb | **S**uccess **b**ound |
| 83 Bismuth | Bi | **Bi**shops |

## CHALCOGENS GROUP 16

| | | |
|---|---|---|
| 8 Oxygen | O | **O**bedience |
| 16 Sulfur | S | **S**tewardship |
| 34 Selenium | Se | **Se**rvant |
| 52 Tellurium | Te | **Te**mperance |
| 84 Polonium | Po | **Po**ndering |

## HALOGENS GROUP 17

| | | |
|---|---|---|
| 9 Fluorine | F | **F**aithfulness |
| 17 Chlorine | Cl | **C**onsistent **l**oyalty |
| 35 Bromine | Br | **Br**otherhood |
| 53 Iodine | I | **I**ntegrity |
| 85 Astatine | At | **At**onement |

## NOBLE (INERT) GASES GROUP 18

|  | | |
|---|---|---|
| 2 Helium | He | **He**aven |
| 10 Neon | Ne | **Ne**w Creation |
| 18 Argon | Ar | **Ar**dor |
| 36 Krypton | Kr | **K**inetic **r**everence |
| 54 Xenon | Xe | **Xe**nophilia |
| 86 Radon | Rn | **R**ighteous **n**eighbor |

# APPENDIX TWO
# PERIODIC CHART ALPHABETICAL
# LIST OF VIRTUES

| VIRTUES: | NUMBER: |
|---|---|
| **Ac**countable | 89 |
| **A**ffirming **s**pirit | 33 |
| **Ag**reeable | 47 |
| **Al**mighty God | 13 |
| **Ar**dor | 18 |
| **At**onement | 85 |
| **Au**thentic | 79 |
| | |
| **Ba**lance | 56 |
| **Be**lief | 4 |
| **Bi**shops | 83 |
| **B**lessings | 5 |
| **Br**otherhood | 35 |

| | |
|---|---|
| **M**oral **n**orms | 25 |
| **Mo**rality | 42 |
| **M**ountain of **G**od | 12 |
| | |
| **Na**vigate God | 11 |
| **N**ear us | 7 |
| **Ne**w creation | 10 |
| **Ni**ce | 28 |
| **N**on-**d**estructive | 60 |
| **N**ot **b**oasting | 41 |
| | |
| **O**bedience | 8 |
| **Os**tracize | 76 |
| | |
| **Pa**radise | 91 |
| **Pd**-in-full | 46 |
| **P**erfect **b**ook | 82 |
| **Po**ndering | 84 |
| **P**rayer **t**ime | 78 |
| **P**rayerful | 15 |
| **P**ro-**m**agnanimous | 61 |
| **Pr**udence | 59 |
| | |
| **Ra**diate | 88 |
| **R**adical **h**umility | 45 |
| **Re**verence | 75 |
| **R**ighteous **b**eing | 37 |
| **R**ighteous **n**eighbor | 86 |
| **Ru**thlike | 44 |
| | |
| **Sc**holars for the Lord | 21 |
| **S**ervant | 34 |

# APPENDIX THREE:
# CHEMICAL PRESENTATION OF THE
# PERIODIC TABLE OF THE ELEMENTS

## The Periodic Table of Elements

| 1 | 2 | | | | | | | | | | | 3 (13) | 4 (14) | 5 (15) | 6 (16) | 7 (17) | 8 (18) |
|---|---|---|---|---|---|---|---|---|---|---|---|---|---|---|---|---|---|
| H 1 | | | | | | | | | | | | | | | | | He 2 |
| Li 3 | Be 4 | | | | | | | | | | | B 5 | C 6 | N 7 | O 8 | F 9 | Ne 10 |
| Na 11 | Mg 12 | (3) | (4) | (5) | (6) | (7) | (8) | (9) | (10) | (11) | (12) | Al 13 | Si 14 | P 15 | S 16 | Cl 17 | Ar 18 |
| K 19 | Ca 20 | Sc 21 | Ti 22 | V 23 | Cr 24 | Mn 25 | Fe 26 | Co 27 | Ni 28 | Cu 29 | Zn 30 | Ga 31 | Ge 32 | As 33 | Se 34 | Br 35 | Kr 36 |
| Rb 37 | Sr 38 | Y 39 | Zr 40 | Nb 41 | Mo 42 | Tc 43 | Ru 44 | Rh 45 | Pd 46 | Ag 47 | Cd 48 | In 49 | Sn 50 | Sb 51 | Te 52 | I 53 | Xe 54 |
| Cs 55 | Ba 56 | La 57 | Hf 72 | Ta 73 | W 74 | Re 75 | Os 76 | Ir 77 | Pt 78 | Au 79 | Hg 80 | Tl 81 | Pb 82 | Bi 83 | Po 84 | At 85 | Rn 86 |
| Fr 87 | Ra 88 | Ac 89 | Rf 104 | Db 105 | Sg 106 | Bh 107 | Hs 108 | Mt 109 | Uun 110 | Uuu 111 | Uub 112 | 113 | Uuq 114 | 115 | 116 | 117 | |

| Ce 58 | Pr 59 | Nd 60 | Pm 61 | Sm 62 | Eu 63 | Gd 64 | Tb 65 | Dy 66 | Ho 67 | Er 68 | Tm 69 | Yb 70 | Lu 71 |
|---|---|---|---|---|---|---|---|---|---|---|---|---|---|
| Th 90 | Pa 91 | U 92 | Np 93 | Pu 94 | Am 95 | Cm 96 | Bk 97 | Cf 98 | Es 99 | Fm 100 | Md 101 | No 102 | Lr 103 |

CPSIA information can be obtained at www.ICGtesting.com
Printed in the USA
BVOW05s1407040614

355386BV00001B/260/P